**New Computing
Environments:
Microcomputers in
Large-Scale Computing**

Proceedings of a Workshop on Microcomputers in Large-Scale Computing, University of Delaware, Newark, Delaware, May 20–22, 1985.

This workshop was sponsored by the U.S. Army Research Office with the assistance and cooperation of the Departments of Computer Science and Mathematics, University of Delaware.

The views presented here are not necessarily those of the United States Army Research Office.

New Computing Environments: Microcomputers in Large-Scale Computing

EDITED BY
Arthur Wouk
U.S. Army Research Office

siam
Philadelphia 1987

Library of Congress Catalog Card Number 87-60442
ISBN 0-89871-210-6

Preface

The papers in this book were presented at a research workshop on Microcomputers in Large-Scale Scientific Computing, which was held at the University of Delaware, Newark, Delaware, on May 20-22, 1985, under the sponsorship of the Army Research Office with the assistance and cooperation of the Departments of Computer Science and Mathematics.

The advent of the relatively inexpensive microcomputer and the related scientific workstation has opened a new era in scientific computation. In this workshop the speakers addressed both the potential and limitations of this new tool and the computing environment which it permits.

In one aspect of this new environment, individual mathematicians, scientists, and engineers can have at their sole and immediate command a potentially powerful tool for numerical mathematics that can be connected easily to larger computers and computing networks. The potential computational power of the hardware available in a microcomputer or workstation is as great as that available on many mainframes not too long ago. If that potential could be realized, individual researchers would no longer be subject to the turn-around delays of batch-processing computer service organizations. They would also be able to avoid the slow responses frequently encountered with time-shared machines, which tend to get bogged down when significant compilations or intensive numerical calculations are required. This new environment also offers more flexibility. When local microcomputers or workstations become available as mathematical tools, it will be possible for researchers to schedule their computing so as to use both the machinery and their own time in a more rational manner than is now possible. As a result, the scientific productivity of scientists, engineers, and mathematicians, working alternately at their local stations for development and testing, and remotely for production,

v

could be improved significantly. Lastly, the costs of computing—both fictitious and real — would be brought within manageable limits.

Two intriguing possibilities on a larger scale that this environment offers are, first, that it is possible to produce, at a relatively modest cost, a collection of independent processors that may be linked together to form an experimental multiprocessor, one which is a model and testbed for the next generation of multi-processor mainframes. Again, this potential calls for many developments in software and algorithmic analysis. Second with these machines there is an increased likelihood that the mainframe a researcher will interact with will be a very remote supercomputer, which raises many questions about data transmission and networking problems.

At the present time, although the potential for this environment is clearly realized, enabling software simply does not exist, and we know only the outlines of what would be needed to achieve it. True, scientific workstations with considerable power do exist, but their cost makes it unlikely that many will soon be available to the community of numerical analysts and other scientists who perform large scale scientific calculation. The more modest microcomputer will be much more prevalent.

The intent of the organizers of the workshop was to bring together a mixture of people who have been addressing the various aspects described above. The sessions were used to introduce the diverse interests of the participants to the group as a whole. In this volume we collect the contributions of eleven of the speakers to the workshop in the order in which the talks were given.

If the microcomputer is to be used as a testbed for more powerful machines, then it is necessary that the same program be compilable and hence runnable over a relatively wide class of machines. **William J. Cody** of Argonne National Laboratories describes his work on SPECFUN, a collection of transportable special function programs (of essentially uniform accuracy) written in FORTRAN, which is capable of running on machines that range from modest microcomputers with FORTRAN compilers to supercomputers. This is a stepping stone toward the ability to run the same program on hardware with a wide range of capabilities.

C. T. Kelley of North Carolina State University describes algorithmic and other considerations in the application of Newton-like methods to problems with singular and near-singular Frechet derivatives, with developmental work performed entirely on microcomputers. The experimental work is demonstrated through approximate solution of the Chandrasekhar H-equation.

William Gropp of Yale University describes CLAM, a system for numerical linear algebra which provides an environment for moving from pilot studies to quality FORTRAN programs on both workstations and mainframes.

Victor L. Pereyra of Weidlinger Associates describes algorithms for ray-tracing in a piecewise homogeneous medium with curved layer interfaces typical of seismic problems. These algorithms have been implemented on a microcomputer as part of a complete modeling system to aid the interpreter of seismic reflection surveys.

George C. Hsiao and **Peter B. Monk** of the University of Delaware implement numerical methods for singular perturbation problems on the microcomputer. An initial value problem for a linear parabolic equation with small parameter is used as a model problem. In order to permit solution on a microcomputer, a modification of the Crank-Nicholson method is developed using methods of asymptotic analysis. Results competitive with mainframe computations are exhibited.

David M. Gay of AT&T Bell Laboratories considers the software problems involved in making use of a large library, the PORT 3 subroutine library, on machines of the personal computer type. This is a large library of over 1500 modules and 4 megabytes of source code. He describes certain tools that make the use of this library on minimal machines "easy."

W. Morven Gentleman of the National Research Council of Canada is developing HARMONY: an operating system for multiprocessors that is based on the Motorola 68000 family of microprocessors connected by commercially available bus structures, and that is capable of supporting standard higher level languages. The HARMONY system is portable to other microprocessor families.

Martin H. Schultz of Yale University has studied bus-connected microprocessor configurations called Linear Array Processors (LAP). He studies as model problems the two-dimensional FFT and two-dimensional filtering and analyzes their performance as the hardware parameters of the configuration are modified. A major conclusion is the importance of algorithmic analysis in designing and using such architectures.

John E. Dennis and **Daniel J. Woods** of Rice University gave a coupled pair of talks about optimization on microcomputers and workstations. The problem addressed is that of minimizing a function of one variable, and the Nelder-Mead algorithm is explored, as one well-suited to microcomputers. Algorithmic studies and interactive graphical implementations are described.

Oliver A. McBryan of the Courant Institute of Mathematical Sciences addresses the issues involved in relating workstations, local mainframes, and remote supercomputers into an effective computational instrument. The talk is represented by two papers, one describing a system for the use of a supercomputer as an attached processor to the local workstation, and the second addressing the problem of developing a software interface to the supercomputer.

Ridgway Scott, then of the University of Michigan and currently at Pennsylvania State University, describes a methodology for evaluation of the useful parameters of a local workstation in light of needs, desires, applications, and finances.

The microcomputer and scientific workstation are continuously changing pieces of hardware. Performance is increasing very rapidly, without any corresponding substantial increase in cost, (in fact the obverse may be true - performance is increasing while cost is decreasing). However, the principles which lead to the work described here remain valid, and these papers show that the office computer of the scientific researcher is capable of being more than just a word processor. It will instead increasingly be the starting point of investigations and the link with more powerful production centers of computation.

Arthur Wouk
U.S Army Research Office

List of Contributors

W. J. Cody, *Mathematics and Computer Science Division, Argonne National Laboratory, Argonne, Illinois 60439*

John E. Dennis, Jr., *Mathematical Sciences Department, Rice University, Houston, Texas 77251*

David M. Gay, *AT&T Bell Laboratories, Murray Hill, New Jersey 07974*

W. Morven Gentleman, *National Research Council of Canada, Ottawa, Ontario, Canada K1A OR8*

William Gropp, *Department of Computer Science, Yale University, New Haven, Connecticut 06520*

George C. Hsiao, *Department of Mathematical Sciences, University of Delaware, Newark, Delaware 19716*

C. T. Kelley, *Department of Mathematics, North Carolina State University, Raleigh, North Carolina 27695*

Oliver A. McBryan, *Los Alamos National Laboratory, Los Alamos, New Mexico 87545*

Peter B. Monk, *Department of Mathematical Sciences, University of Delaware, Newark, Delaware 19716*

V. Pereyra, *Weidlinger Associates, Palo Alto, California 94304*

Martin H. Schultz, *Research Center for Scientific Computation, Yale University, New Haven, Connecticut 06520*

L. Ridgway Scott, *Department of Mathematics, University of Michigan, Ann Arbor, Michigan 48109*

Daniel J. Woods, *Mathematical Sciences Department, Rice University, Houston, Texas 77251*

Contents

SPECFUN: A Portable Special Function Package

W. J. CODY*

   Abstract.   SPECFUN is a collection of transportable Fortran
special function programs and accompanying test drivers that is
currently under development.   Elements of the package have been
successfully run on machines as diverse in characteristics as a
Kaypro II, an IBM PC, a VAX 11/780, an IBM 3033, and a Cray-1.   This
is a discussion of the overall capabilities, design characteristics,
and implementation details of the package.

   1.   Introduction. The FUNPACK package of Fortran special function
programs [Cody, 1975, 1984] developed in the 1970s was noted for its
accuracy, reliability, robustness, and complete lack of portability.
While the package is still used on the machines for which it was
designed, it can not be used on many of the new machines that have
appeared over the last decade.   SPECFUN is a new package of Fortran
special function programs that is designed with transportability as
the overriding attribute.   Ultimately SPECFUN will contain counterparts for all of the special function programs in FUNPACK as well as
programs for functions not included in FUNPACK.   In addition, the
package will contain completely portable test drivers, patterned
after those in ELEFUNT [Cody and Waite, 1980], that will be capable
of testing any special function programs with functionalities and
calling sequences corresponding to those in SPECFUN.

   The successful design of a special function package necessarily
involves   compromises   among   efficiency,   reliability,   robustness,
transportability, and achievable accuracy.   Section 2 discusses the
design problem and the particular compromises made for SPECFUN.
Section 3 describes the testing philosophy and some of the test
programs.   Finally, section 4 discusses the present contents of the
package and future plans.

*Mathematics   and   Computer   Science   Division,   Argonne   National
Laboratory, Argonne, IL 60439.   This work was supported by the
Applied Mathematical Sciences subprogram of the Office of Energy
Research, U.S. Department of Energy, under contract W-31-109-Eng-38.

2.   <u>Design Characteristics</u>.   Two major considerations in the preparation of special function software are the selection of an algorithm, and the details of the implementation of that algorithm. The quality of the implementation is reflected in attributes of reliability, robustness, and transportability that are nearly, but not entirely, independent of the algorithm. We will see shortly that these attributes are not always compatible with one another, and some compromises are necessary in the overall design of a function package.

Because these software attributes have been discussed many times in the open literature, we will limit our discussion here to a definition of each and perhaps a simple illustration. <u>Reliability</u> refers to the ability of the software to obtain desired computational results accurately and efficiently.   To the extent that a poor algorithm may limit both accuracy and efficiency, this property does depend on the quality of the algorithm being implemented, although that dependence is sometimes filtered out of the definition.   A strict definition refers only to whether the software is faithful to the underlying algorithm, i.e., whether the software approaches the limits on accuracy and efficiency imposed by the algorithm. We use the broader definition here in the belief that nobody would be satisfied with the performance of a subroutine for the exponential function,   or example,   that simply evaluated the Taylor series expansion.   No matter how faithful the implementation was, the inherent severe cancellation error for large arguments would not be acceptable.   Algorithms used in   SPECFUN are selected to maximize performance; hence, the only reliability issues we face are related to implementation.   The distinction between the strict and broad definitions of reliability are not important in this case.

The second attribute is <u>robustness</u>, the resiliency of a program under improper or unwise use.   A linear equations solver that accepts a negative integer for the order of a system of equations, without complaint, is clearly defective and dangerous.   It lacks robustness even if it performs flawlessly when the parameters are correctly specified.   In the case of special function programs, lack of robustness probably is most often associated with a lack of protection against intermediate underflow and overflow, although lack of protection against invalid arguments is also common. Program authors sometimes make no effort to avoid underflow because they assume first that the host computer system quietly replaces underflow with zero and continues computation, and second that such an action has no adverse affect on their computation.   These are dangerous assumptions, especially if the program is to be transported to unknown systems that may signal an exception or stop execution when underflow is encountered. Even if computation continues, the default numerical result may not be zero. Depending on the particular system, it could be the algebraically smallest positive number (perhaps with the correct sign), or it could be something completely unexpected, such as the <u>largest</u> machine number.   Because the possible consequences of underflow are so varied, and often so unpleasant, we have chosen to avoid them in SPECFUN whenever it is reasonable to do so.

Finally, there is the attribute of transportability. We say that software is <u>portable</u> if it can be moved from one system to any other system without change and without degradation in performance. We say it is <u>transportable</u> if it can be so moved with only small, well-documented changes. There are few, if any, truly portable programs of any kind. In the case of special function programs, the degree of transportability depends on certain language issues (we must restrict ourselves to some universally accepted subset of a standardized programming language), on the algorithm, and on the mechanism for expressing machine-dependent quantities. We will see in a moment that other, more subtle factors also influence transportability.

If there is a unifying concept behind the properties of reliability, robustness, and transportability, it is that they each involve detailed interaction with the computational environment. Consider the task of writing a Fortran program for the evaluation of the Bessel function $I_1(x)$. For small x,

$$I_1(x) = x/2$$

to machine precision, so there is a machine-dependent threshold below which an efficient program would replace whatever computation is being used with x/2. Of course, x/2 < x, so there is a second threshold below which this computation produces underflow. This second threshold is very close to the smallest positive floating-point number, and relatively few offending arguments will be filtered out by testing against this threshold. Is such a test worthwhile? For a completely robust program, it is not only worthwhile, it is necessary by definition.

There are other considerations, however. While the value of the threshold used in the first case is not critical as long as it is a conservative value, the value of the underflow threshold must be exact. This means that it not only is machine-dependent, but it must be represented in the native representation for the machine. Clearly, such a requirement is detrimental to portability. But the situation is even worse. On some machines, including large Univac machines, testing a floating-point value against a threshold involves subtraction. If such machines are not to introduce underflow in the very test intended to avoid it, the threshold and the value being tested must be carefully scaled, introducing yet another machine-dependent constant (this time for scaling), an unusual machine-dependent program segment, and more impediments to portability.

This situation is not unique. Similar problems arise with Dawson's integral, for example, where asymptotically

$$F(x) \sim 1/2x, \quad x \to \infty .$$

On some machines, $1/2x$ exists for all $x>1$, while on others, there exist large x for which it does not exist. Thus, on some equipment it is necessary to include a machine-dependent threshold and test that is not needed on other equipment.

These examples illustrate the fundamental conflict between performance and robustness on the one hand, and transportability on the other. Certain decisions about the relative importance of these attributes must be made early in the design of software, and implementors must adhere to them. FUNPACK, for example, chose performance and robustness over transportability. The programs in that package are extremely reliable and well protected against system-generated exceptions, but they are also extremely machine-dependent. In contrast, SPEC FUN has accepted some penalties in performance and robustness to achieve transportability. The SPEC FUN program for $I_1(x)$, for example, contains no threshold for small x, trading the transportability problems just discussed for a minute risk that underflow may occur for extremely small arguments. By our definitions, this one omission means that this particular program lacks robustness even though it performs well in every other respect. It is our intention in SPEC FUN that where robustness must be sacrificed for portability, it will be at about this level of severity. We have not yet found a satisfactory solution to the dilemma we face with Dawson's integral.

There remain the questions of algorithm selection and implementation details that depend on such characteristics of floating-point systems as wordlength. In general, SPEC FUN programs follow the lead of FUNPACK by using rational minimax approximations for functions of one argument and recurrence algorithms for functions of two or more variables. The program GAMMA for $\Gamma(x)$, for example, implements an algorithm outlined in Cody [1976] using one unpublished approximation generated especially for this program, and several other approximations taken from Hart et al. [1968]. On the other hand, the program RIBESL [Cody, 1983] for the general Bessel function $I_\nu(x)$ for real ν and x is based on an earlier program by Sookne [1973]. It uses a modification of the familiar three-term recurrence scheme associated with Miller. When SPEC FUN programs like RIBESL are based on public domain software, the 'value added' is primarily in the enhancement of the software attributes discussed above, and in the imposition of programming conventions to be described next.

To further promote portability, programs based on approximations use the same approximations for all machines, with accuracy targeted at about 20 significant decimal places. This means that the programs are inefficient on some machines, evaluating approximations that are too accurate, while they are constrained by the 20S accuracy on other machines. Coefficients and many other numerical values supplied with a program are specified in decimal to about 20S. This trades enhanced portability for a small conversion error at compile time. Exceptions to this 20S rule are certain thresholds and non-critical constants where less precise values are acceptable, or even desirable.

Wherever possible, error thresholds and other machine dependencies are expressed in terms of common machine parameters, such as the radix, wordlength, and extreme exponents. In a few cases, machine-dependent quantities can only be described as the solution to nonlinear equations involving machine parameters. For example,

$$\Gamma(x) \gg x, \quad x \gg 1 \ .$$

To determine XMAX, the largest acceptable argument for GAMMA for a particular machine, we must solve the equation

$$\Gamma(XMAX) = XINF \ ,$$

where XINF is the largest finite floating-point number on the machine. This is converted to a more tractable equation by using logs:

$$\ln\Gamma(XMAX) = maxexp \times \ln(b) \ ,$$

where b is the radix for the system, and maxexp is the largest floating-point exponent. This last equation can be solved for almost any selection of machine parameters on a machine of even modest range. Simply replace $\Gamma(x)$ with a few terms of Stirling's formula, and apply Newton iteration. Given the machine parameters for a set of machines, it is possible to determine the corresponding machine-dependent parameters for any particular function program using schemes like this. Predetermined parameters for a selection of popular machines are included in COMMENTs at the top of SPECFUN programs. Conversion of a program for a particular machine is then a simple matter of determining the proper parameter values, either from the COMMENTs or by using the definitions supplied, and inserting them in DATA statements.

All coefficients and mathematical constants are specified in DATA statements; no decimal constants occur in executable statements. This helps localize the changes needed to convert from one precision to another. That conversion has been further simplified by duplicat-ing all precision-dependent declarations and executable statements with the obvious changes. Statements peculiar to single precision contain CS' in the first two columns, while their immediately following counterparts for double precision contain CD'. It is then a matter of doing a global search and replace operation on the first two columns of a source file to produce a precision-specific version of a program. Because Fortran 66 compilers are still quite common, SPECFUN programs do not yet rely on the generic intrinsic functions provided in Fortran 77. That design decision may be modified short-ly, however. The version of SPECFUN that has been particularized for the IBM/PC is already an exception to this rule.

Ultimately, the quality and transportability of a numerical software package such as SPECFUN depends on how well the author understood and dealt with constraints imposed by arithmetic systems and compilers. He must understand the constraints not only for the equipment used to develop the programs, but also for any equipment to which they might be moved. That is a great responsibility, and one reason little truly transportable numerical software exists. It is also a reason that claims for transportability, even those associated with SPECFUN, must be viewed suspiciously.

3. __Test Package.__ A unique component of SPECFUN is the set of transportable, self-contained test programs similar in concept to those in ELEFUNT. The test programs are designed in the belief that the ideal evaluation of a program should be in the spirit of a physical examination. That is, the testing procedures followed should be thorough, checking robustness as well as accuracy, and should discover both strengths and weaknesses of programs under test. The test programs should be general enough to be used on any function programs with calling sequences and functionalities matching those of the SPECFUN programs. Finally, they should be written with the same care and attention to detail as any other element of SPECFUN.

Accuracy testing requires finesse if the program under test is truly good. Any testing procedure, even comparison against tables, will quickly pick out programs that are correct to only two or three digits; subtle and sophisticated procedures are necessary to demonstrate accuracy to within a few rounding errors on the host machine. By far the best procedure for such testing is a controlled comparison against higher-precision computations within the machine. Such techniques are not acceptable for SPECFUN, however, because they are machine-dependent, and difficult to use when the function being tested already uses the highest precision available. Instead, SPECFUN accuracy tests use carefully selected and programmed identities whenever possible. The resulting accuracy statistics are useful, but not as discriminating as those obtained by comparison against higher-precision computations. That is the main penalty for transportability.

As an example, we present the procedure for testing the accuracy of programs to evaluate $\ln\Gamma(x)$. First, we select an identity that involves no other function, is numerically stable for an interesting range of arguments, and is not likely to be an essential component of any software evaluating the function (Wronskians and recurrence relations are therefore poor choices for testing Bessel programs). The identity selected in this case is the duplication formula (Equation 6.1.18 in Abramowitz and Stegun [1964]):

$$\ln\Gamma(2x) = -\ln(\sqrt{2\pi}) + (2x-1/2)\ln(2) + \ln\Gamma(x) + \ln\Gamma(x+1/2) \ .$$

Useful restatements of this relation are obtained by replacing x with x/2, and x-1/2, respectively.

Using the original formulation, we find

$$\ln\Gamma(x) = \ln(2\sqrt{\pi}) - y\,\ln(2) + \ln\Gamma(y) - \ln\Gamma(z) ,$$

where $y = 2x$ and $z = x+1/2$. To estimate the relative error in $\ln\Gamma(x)$, we evaluate the expression

$$E = \frac{\ln\Gamma(x) - [\ln(2\sqrt{\pi}) - y\,\ln(2) + \ln\Gamma(y) - \ln\Gamma(z)]}{\ln\Gamma(x)} .$$

Assume that δ denotes the relative error in the computed value of $\ln\Gamma(x)$, d that in $\ln\Gamma(y)$, and e that in $\ln\Gamma(z)$. Further assume that x, y, and z are <u>exactly</u> representable in the machine, hence contribute no error to the computation. This condition is achieved through a process called argument purification which we will illustrate in a moment. Then, ignoring higher-order terms in the errors, elementary algebra shows that,

$$E \approx \delta - M_1 d + M_2 e ,$$

where

$$M_1 = \frac{\ln\Gamma(y)}{\ln\Gamma(x)} ,$$

and

$$M_2 = \frac{\ln\Gamma(z)}{\ln\Gamma(x)} .$$

Simple computation shows that $|M_1| < 1.4$ for $x < 0.875$, and $|M_2| < 1$ for $x < 0.8799$. Therefore, the identity is well behaved and measures δ with acceptably small contamination for $0 < x < 0.875$, say. Note that the quantities $\ln(2\sqrt{\pi})$ and $\ln(2)$ are mathematical constants known to arbitrary precision. Terms involving these quantities can be introduced into the computation with essentially no error using procedures similar to those used in determining reduced arguments in elementary function programs [Cody, 1982].

There remains the question of how to purify the arguments to remove any rounding error. That is accomplished in this case by the following sequence of Fortran statements:

```
Z = X + HALF
X = Z - HALF
Y = X + X
```

where HALF has the value 0.5 and X is assumed to be random in the interval [0,0.875]. The first two statements are the key to this purification. They introduce a zero in the low-order digit of the significand of X whenever the machine representation of Z carries a larger exponent than that for X, regardless of the radix for the representation. Even though the computed value of Z may involve rounding, thus destroying the mathematical relation between Z and the original value of X, the recomputed value of X is free of rounding, restoring the mathematical relation. Because X was random, the possible perturbation of its low order digit does no damage. The final computation of Y cannot cause an exponent adjustment for the selected range of X unless that adjustment has already been induced by the computation of Z. The final computed values of X, Y and Z therefore have the required mathematical properties.

Tests for other intervals are constructed from the previously mentioned variable transformations in the original identity. Analysis similar to the above determines different error amplification coefficients M_1 and M_2, and consideration of bounds on those coefficients determines the test intervals. The details of argument purification also differ. But none of these details are any more difficult to derive than what has just been done.

How effective are the tests? The driver has been used to test a representative selection of programs for $\ln\Gamma(x)$ on several different machines. Table 1 gives results for tests run on a VAX 11/780 under Unix, and on an IBM PC running DOS 2.0 and Microsoft Fortran 3.2. The other programs tested came from the NAG library [Ford and Pool, 1984], the IMSL library [Aird, 1984], and FNLIB, a public-domain predecessor of SFUN [IMSL, 1984]. The "calibration" figures were

Table 1. Test Results for Single Precision $\ln\Gamma(x)$
on VAX 11/780 and IBM PC

| | Test Intervals | | | | | |
| Code | (0.0, 0.9) | | (1.3, 1.6) | | (2.2, 20.0) | |
	MRE	RMS	MRE	RMS	MRE	RMS
VAX 11/780:						
Calibration	1.02	0.00	1.77	0.00	2.40	0.00
SPECFUN/ALGAMA	2.33	0.18	2.17	0.45	2.55	0.32
NAG/S14ABF	2.86	1.38	3.78	3.24	2.11	0.29
IMSL/ALGAMA	3.78	1.46	3.62	2.52	3.36	1.11
FNLIB/ALNGAM	4.41	1.48	4.29	2.75	3.65	0.17
IBM PC:						
Calibration	1.00	0.00	1.77	0.00	1.00	0.00
SPECFUN/ALGAMA	2.09	0.03	1.77	0.22	1.89	0.04

obtained by testing a single-precision program that did all computations in double precision, returning a correctly rounded single-precision result. Thus, these figures measure the performance of the test program on an "ideal" function program, i.e., they approximate the error introduced by the testing process.

The statistics quoted are the maximum relative error, MRE, and root mean square relative error, RMS, for a sample of 2000 random arguments uniformly distributed across each test interval. Errors are measured in units of the least significant digit of the floating-point significand (ULPs). This measurement permits some comparison of performance across machine lines because it is independent of the machine word length. Note the consistency in the results of tests of similar programs on the two different machines.

We caution against making unwarranted comparisons based solely on this table. The results reported represent only one instance of an accuracy test. They should not be extrapolated to imply anything about the comparative quality of the libraries sampled, nor even of the individual programs tested. They do indicate which of the programs warrant additional investigation and which might be further improved in accuracy. They also indicate that the SPECFUN program performs well. Emphasizing the positive, none of the programs tested exhibits unacceptable accuracy.

Not all of the test programs in SPECFUN rely on identities for accuracy testing, however. In cases where suitable identities have not been found, we must resort to other means. For example, the test program for $I_0(x)$ compares against numerically stable analytic expansions for small x, and against values generated using the program for $I_\nu(x)$ when x is large. The results of such comparisons could be misleading if the program under test used essentially the same methods for its computations. That is not the case with SPECFUN programs, but it may render a few of the test programs unreliable for checking functions from other libraries.

The remaining task is to check a program's robustness. Designing tests for this requires imagination. It is not difficult to unintentionally misuse a program, but it is impossible to anticipate all possible misuses or programming omissions ahead of time. The tests in SPECFUN are limited to the checks that have come to mind, and are assuredly incomplete. For example, we overlooked a test for underflow for very small arguments in $I_1(x)$ until we prepared the discussion of the underflow threshold presented in the last section. This additional check probes a weakness in the SPECFUN program, but is consistent with the analogy between testing and physical examinations made earlier. We believe our test programs check all of the obvious misuses involving illegal arguments and arguments at and beyond the various thresholds. These thresholds must be computed within the test program. That is not difficult, as we saw above in the discussion of the determination of the overflow threshold for the

gamma function. There are some obvious omissions in the tests. We
have not tested programs with more than one parameter to see what
happens if more than one is incorrect, or if one is completely
missing.

Of necessity, many of the test programs in the SPECFUN package
need correct values for the machine parameters mentioned earlier.
These are obtained dynamically with the MACHAR program from ELEFUNT.
MACHAR computes machine parameters from a built-in model of the
arithmetic system. It will malfunction on machines, such as those
based on IEEE style arithmetic [Cody, et al., 1984], that use an
incompatible model. Accurate values of the machine parameters must
be determined by other means for such machines.

4. Package Contents and Plans. Table 2 contrasts the contents of
FUNPACK with the contents of SPECFUN as of April 1, 1985. The
ordering and general notation of the functions follows those of
Abramowitz and Stegun [1964]. All variables and parameters are
real. An "X" indicates that the "final" program exists and a "P"
indicates that a "prototype" program exists.

Eventually SPECFUN will contain programs and test drivers for
every function in the table, and for functions such as $Y_0(x)$ and
$Y_1(x)$ to fill the obvious gaps. In a few cases, prototype programs
and test drivers already exist. Some of these additions are needed
for use with the test drivers for existing programs. The test
drivers for $K_0(x)$ and $K_1(x)$, for example, now test accuracy for large
arguments by comparing against results from a prototype $K_\nu(x)$. While
the prototype program is already good enough for this purpose, it is
not yet good enough for general use. Eventually, we plan to include
useful functions not in the table, such as Fresnel integrals, the
Riemann zeta function, repeated integrals of the error function, and
the higher exponential integrals. We want to expand the coverage to
functions of complex argument, especially Bessel functions and the
gamma-related functions, but that work has lower priority than the
work for the real functions.

Early versions of two SPECFUN programs, RIBESL for $I_\nu(x)$ and GAMMA
for $\Gamma(x)$, have been published [Cody, 1983]. All of the programs
completed so far have been particularized for the IBM/PC by embedding
appropriate machine-dependent constants, stripping out all references
to parameters for other machines, and using the Fortran 77 generic
intrinsic and elementary functions. Some of these latter programs
are found in the Scientific Desk [C. Abaci, 1984]. Those for $\Gamma(x)$,
$\ln\Gamma(x)$, $erf(x)$, $I_0(x)$, $I_1(x)$, and $I_\nu(x)$ will soon be available on
diskette from the National Energy Software Center at Argonne National
Laboratory. Because these programs are all in the public domain,
they will also be available through other sources such as the Netlib
distribution over Arpanet/CSNET [Dongarra and Grosse, 1985].

Table 2.   Contents of FUNPACK and SPECFUN

Function	FUNPACK Function Program	SPECFUN Function Program	SPECFUN Test Program
$E_1(x),Ei(x),e^{-x}Ei(x)$	X		
$\Gamma(x)$		X	X
$\ln\Gamma(x)$		X	X
$\psi(x)$	X		
$erf(x),erfc(x)$		X	
$F(x)$	X		
$J_0(x)$ X	X	X	P
$J_1(x)$ X	X	X	P
$J_\nu(x)$		P	P
$Y_\nu(x)$	X		
$I_0(x),e^{-x}I_0(x)$	X	X	X
$I_1(x),e^{-x}I_1(x)$	X	X	X
$I_\nu(x),e^{-x}I_\nu(x)$		X	X
$K_0(x),e^xK_0(x)$	X	X	P
$K_1(x),e^xK_1(x)$	X	X	P
$K_\nu(x),e^xK_\nu(x)$		P	P
$K(m),K(k),K(\eta)$	X		
$E(m),E(k),E(\eta)$	X		

REFERENCES

M. ABRAMOWITZ and I. A. STEGUN [1964].   Handbook of Mathematical Functions with Formulas, Graphs, and Mathematical Tables, National Bureau of Standards Applied Mathematics Series Vol. 55, U.S. Government Printing Office, Washington, D.C.

T. J. AIRD [1984].   The IMSL library, in Sources and Development of Mathematical Software, Ed. W. R. Cowell, Prentice-Hall, Englewood Cliffs, New Jersey, pp. 264-301.

C. ABACI, INC. [1984].   The Scientific Desk, C. Abaci, Raleigh, North Carolina.

W. J. CODY [1975]. The FUNPACK package of special function routines, ACM Trans. on Math. Soft. 1, pp. 13–25.

W. J. CODY [1976]. An overview of software development for special functions, in Numerical Analysis Dundee 1975, Ed. A. Dold and B. Eckmann. Springer-Verlag, New York, pp. 38–48.

W. J. CODY [1982]. Implementation and testing of function software, in Problems and Methodologies in Mathematical Software Production, Ed. P. C. Messina and A. Murli. Springer-Verlag, New York, pp. 24–47.

W. J. CODY [1983]. Algorithm 597: Sequence of modified Bessel functions of the first kind, ACM Trans. on Math. Soft. 9, pp. 242–245.

W. J. CODY [1984]. FUNPACK – a package of special function routines, in Sources and Development of Mathematical Software, Ed. W. R. Cowell. Prentice-Hall, Englewood Cliffs, New Jersey, pp. 49–67.

W. J. CODY, J. T. COONEN, D. M. GAY, K. HANSON, D. HOUGH, W. KAHAN, R. KARPINSKI, J. PALMER, F. N. RIS, and D. STEVENSON [1984]. A proposed radix- and wordlength-independent standard for floating-point arithmetic, IEEE Micro. 4(4), pp. 86–100.

W. J. CODY and W. WAITE [1980]. Software Manual for the Elementary Functions, Prentice-Hall, Englewood Cliffs, New Jersey.

J. J. DONGARRA and E. GROSSE [1985]. Distribution of Mathematical Software by Electronic Mail, Report ANL/MCS-TM-48, Mathematics and Computer Science Division, Argonne National Laboratory, Argonne, Illinois.

B. FORD and J. C. T. POOL [1984]. The evolving NAG library service, in Sources and Development of Mathematical Software, Ed. W. R. Cowell. Prentice-Hall, Englewood Cliffs, New Jersey, pp. 375–397.

J. F. HART, E. W. CHENEY, C. L. LAWSON, H. J. MAEHLY, C. K. MESZTENYI, J. R. RICE, H. C. THACHER, Jr., and C. WITZGALL [1968]. Computer Approximations, John Wiley and Sons, New York.

IMSL [1984]. SFUN/LIBRARY User's Manual, IMSL, Inc., Houston Texas.

D. J. SOOKNE [1973]. Bessel functions of real argument and integer order, in NBS Jour. Res. B, 77A, pp. 125–132.

Algorithm Design on Microcomputers: Newton's Method for Problems with Singular Jacobian

C. T. KELLEY*

Abstract

This paper reports on results on Newton like methods for problems with singular and nearly singular Fréchet derivative obtained by the author and co-workers over a period of several years. The numerical experiments in the beginning were entirely done on microcomputers and, even now, much of the prototyping is done on small computers. The advantages of small computers for experimental work for this kind of problem are discussed and the results are summarized in the context of a specific example, the Chandrasekhar H-equation. The example is easy to program on even a small microcomputer, and the reader can duplicate much of the observations reported.

1. Introduction

This paper is about the author's use of microcomputers for experimentation and how that experimentation led to new mathematical results on the performance of Newton and Newton-like iterative methods for nonlinear equations where the Jacobian is singular at the root. Many of the experiments were done on very small computers, ranging from the HP-97 calculator to the IBM-PC/AT. Without the freedom that microcomputers offer for this type of work, where it is not clear that anything concrete will be produced, much of the results reported in [8−13,23−27] would not exist.

When experiments are being done on moderately small problems, we found that the turnaround time for a microcomputer was far smaller that for a mainframe. On a mainframe the competition with many other users slows the edit-compile-run cycle enough to offset the faster execution time.

---

* Department of Mathematics, Box 8205 North Carolina State Univ. Raleigh, N.C. 27695-8205
This work was supported by NSF grants #DMS-8300841 and #DMS-8500944.

The cost of work on a microcomputer is zero. For work that is largely experimental with a payoff that is uncertain, this is an important advantage.

Microcomputers are small and slow. We did find it necessary to use large machines more and more often as the research progressed. However, we still do most of our prototyping on a microcomputer. Our particular configuration is inexpensive ($<$ \$6000) and outperforms even the large minicomputers on the North Carolina State campus with the typical daytime load. We use an IBM-PC/AT with hardware floating point, C and Fortran compilers, an assembler, and communications software that allows us to move code to larger machines when needed. We have found it helpful to code some common functions (e.g. dot product) in assembler; this task is not as difficult and is more useful than it would be on a larger machine. We observe a 2x speedup in routines like Gaussian elimination. On a machine as slow as our micro, a factor of two is worth some effort.

Most of the observations mentioned in this paper can be made on even a small microcomputer. We do not give tables of the observations; instead, we give sufficient information to allow the reader to make the observations on his or her own microcomputer; to do this one would only need a compiler that supports a double precision data type so as to solve the nearly singular linear problems and do the function evaluations to sufficient accuracy. At the end of the paper we discuss observations made for large problems on a mainframe. Though these could not be made on a microcomputer, the idea of making them in the first place came from small scale work on a small machine.

All the results in this paper are related to solution of the Chandrasekhar H-equation, [5−7], which arises in radiative transfer:

$$H(\mu) = 1 + \frac{c}{2}H(\mu)\int_0^1 \frac{\mu}{\mu+\nu}H(\nu)d\nu . \qquad (1.1)$$

In the equation, H is the unknown function and c is a parameter. Values of $c \in (0,1]$ are of interest. For $0 < c < 1$ there are two solutions of equation (1.1), only one of which has physical meaning, [28]. We shall denote this physically meaningful solution by H; it is characterized by analyticity in the variable c, [23,24,28]. When $c = 1$ there is a unique solution. Aside from its physical interest, the H-equation is a useful testbed for iterative methods because its structure is well understood and there have been tables of accurate values available for years, [1,7]. Moreover, as we will describe later, the algebraic structure of the problem does not change if the integral is approximated by a reasonable quadrature rule, [28].

Equation (1.1) can be rewritten as

$$H - (1-cL(H))^{-1} , \tag{1.2}$$

where L is the integral operator

$$L(f)(\mu) = \tfrac{1}{2}\int_0^1 \frac{\mu}{\mu+\nu} f(\nu)d\nu . \tag{1.3}$$

We will write (1.1) as $F(H) = 0$; (1.2) could also be used and only some minor details would change, [23,24,28]. We will approximate integrals by quadrature rules; the rule used by the author to make his own observations was a composite 20 point Gauss rule. We write the quadrature rule as

$$\sum_{j=1}^N f(x_j)w_j . \tag{1.4}$$

The operator L is approximated by L_N which is given by

$$L_N(f)(\mu) = \tfrac{1}{2}\sum_{j=1}^N \frac{\mu}{\mu+x_j}f(x_j)w_j . \tag{1.5}$$

The approximate nonlinear map, F_N is obtained from F by replacement of L by L_N. If we let H^N be the solution of $F_N(H^N) = 0$ then computation of $H^N(x_j)$ for $1 \le j \le N$ is a finite dimensional problem. When this is solved, one may recover values of H^N at other points by using (1.2). In this way one may test results against the tables.

In what follows we make no distinction between F and F_N. The reason is that if the quadrature rule integrates constant functions exactly, all formulae, statements about null spaces and derivatives, and all convergence rates are the same for both the infinite dimensional problem and its finite dimensional approximation. Likewise we make no distinction between H and H^N. We let F' denote the Fréchet derivative of F. We will understand that F is defined on a Banach space E, which is $C[0,1]$ in the continuous case and R^N in the discrete case.

We conclude this section with a theorem that is a combination of results from [23,24,28]:

Theorem A: *If* $0 < c \le 1$, *then H is an increasing function and* $H(\mu) \ge 1$ *for all* $\mu \in [0,1]$. *Moreover if* $c \ne 1$, $F'(H)$ *is nonsingular on E; if* $c = 1$, $F'(H)$ *has a one dimensional null space, N, which is the span of* μH. *Moreover, if* $c = 1$, *then for all* $u \in C[0,1]$

$$\int_0^1 (F'(H)u)(\mu)d\mu = 0 . \tag{1.6}$$

2. Newton like iterative methods

2.1. Newton's Method

If $c < 1$ and Newton's method is used to compute H, one would expect to see (and does see) quadratic convergence of the Newton iterates to the solution. We see this by observing that the size of the steps,

$$s_n = -F'(H_n)^{-1}F(H_n) \qquad (2.1)$$

decreases quadratically when measured in either the max norm or any L^P norm. Here the initial iterate, H_0 was the function identically equal to one. We will let $\| \; \|$ denote any of these norms. One can also observe that the ratios $\log(\|s_{n+1}\|)/\log(\|s_n\|)$ tend to the q-order of two in this situation.

When $c = 1$ we see that the ratios $\|s_{n+1}\|/\|s_n\|$ tend to ½. This is not surprising in view of the fact that for nonlinear equations in one variable, $f(x) = 0$, for which $f(x^*) = f'(x^*) = 0 \neq f''(x^*)$, the rate of convergence of the Newton iterates is linear with linear ratio ½, if the initial iterate, x_0, is in a sufficiently small deleted neighborhood of the root, $W(\rho)$. Here

$$W(\rho) = \{x \mid |x-x^*| < \rho\} . \qquad (2.2)$$

Note that $W(\rho)$ avoids the set on which $f'(x) = 0$, which is locally the single point, x^*, since $f''(x^*) \neq 0$. However, for higher dimensional problems, the set

$$M = \{x \mid F'(x) \text{ is singular }\} \qquad (2.3)$$

is in general a codimension one smooth manifold through x^*. Hence the initial iterate for Newton's method must be kept away from this set as well as be kept near the root, x^*. For the H-equation, as we observed linear convergence with rate ½, we expect that in some sense the second derivative of F at H satisfies some sort of non-degeneracy condition.

Some general conditions, satisfied by the H-equation, that imply linear convergence to the root with linear rate ½ are summarized in Theorem B, which is a blending of results from [8−10,16,17,32,33]. We shall assume that the following hypotheses hold for F

(1) F is a C^3 map from a Banach space E into itself, $F(x^*) = 0$.

(2) $F'(x^*)$ has a one dimensional null space $N = \text{span}(\phi)$ and range X with $E = N \oplus X$.

(3) If P_N is a projector onto N parallel to X then $P_N F''(x^*)(\phi,\phi) \neq 0$.

The hypothesis, (3), is the high dimensional analog of the condition that $f''(x^*) \neq 0$ for equations in one variable. It's geometric meaning is that the set M, on which F' is singular, has a tangent surface at x^* that is not parallel to ϕ. A consequence of this is that the set $W(\rho,\theta)$ given by

$$W(\rho,\theta) = \{x \mid 0 < ||\tilde{x}|| < \rho , \ ||P_X\tilde{x}|| < \theta||P_N\tilde{x}||\} \tag{2.4}$$

does not intersect M for ρ and θ small enough, [9,16,17,25,27]. A second consequence is that there are no other roots near x^*, [22]. In (2.4), $\tilde{x} = x - x^*$ and $P_X = I - P_N$.

Theorem B: *Assume that $P_NF''(x^*)(\phi,\phi) \neq 0$. Then, if ρ and θ are sufficiently small and $x_0 \in W(\rho,\theta)$, the Newton iterates, $\{x_n\}$, remain in $W(\rho,\theta)$, converge to x^*, and satisfy*

$$\lim_{n \to \infty} \frac{||\tilde{x}_{n+1}||}{||\tilde{x}_n||} = \tfrac{1}{2} , \tag{2.5}$$

and

$$\lim_{n \to \infty} \frac{||P_X\tilde{x}_n||}{||P_N\tilde{x}_n||^2} = 0 . \tag{2.6}$$

The significance of (2.6) has not been explained yet. We will return to it in the next subsection on acceleration of convergence.

We show how the hypotheses (1)-(3) can be verified for the H-equation. (1) is trivial and (2) is a consequence of Theorem (1.6). We check (3). The arguements here use results from Theorem A. We use (1.6) to note that a projection onto N parallel to X can be given by

$$P_N(u)(\mu) = \frac{\displaystyle\int_0^1 u(\nu)d\nu}{\displaystyle\int_0^1 \phi(\nu)d\nu}\phi(\mu) . \tag{2.7}$$

Note that F'' is given, for $u,v \in C[0,1]$ by

$$F''(u,v) = -vLu - uLv . \tag{2.8}$$

Since $\phi \geq 0$ and L is an integral operator with a nonnegative kernel, the function $P_NF''(H)(\phi,\phi)(\mu) < 0$ for $\mu > 0$. This completes the verification of hypotheses (3).

Making sure that the initial iterate lies in $W(\rho,\theta)$ is more difficult. Here we note that since $\phi \geq 0$, an initial iterate, H_0, that was always $\leq$ (or $\geq$) H might be expected to differ from H by an amount with larger N-component that one whose values straddled the values of H. As $H \geq 1$, the function identically one is a reasonable initial guess as far as the direction goes.

It is interesting to note that if c is near 1, the size of the ball about H in which Newton's method converges quadratically will have a much smaller volume than the set $W(\rho,\theta)$. However, Newton's method will converge in a small perturbation of $W(\rho,\theta)$ for such problems, [13], giving a larger convergence set.

Note that the verification of the assumptions used the nonnegativity of the solution, the spanning vector for the null space, and the kernel of the integral operator L. Without structure of this type the assumptions would be much harder to verify.

Finally, one might think that, as in the one variable case, linear rates of the form $k/k+1$, where $k+1$ is the order of the root, are all that can be seen for problems with singular Jacobian. This is not the case and it is not completely clear what one means by the order of a root for an equation with more than one unknown. The assumptions we made for Theorem B, while satisfied for the H-equation, are not general. Very strange convergence behavior has been observed for reasonable looking problems, [18,31].

2.2. Acceleration of Convergence

For nonlinear equations in one variable where the derivative vanishes at the root but $f''(x^*) \neq 0$, the Newton iterates can be modified to recover superlinear convergence by doubling the step at each iteration. The modified iterates

$$x_{n+1} = x_n - 2\frac{f(x)}{f'(x)} , \qquad (2.9)$$

converge quadratically to the root, x^*, provided x_0 is in $W(\rho)$ for ρ sufficiently small, [38].

It is natural to try and do the same thing for nonlinear problems in higher dimensions; this fails. What one sees, at least with the H-equation, is that the iterates seem to converge very erratically to the root. Sometimes an iterate may be tens of times further away than the previous one. There have been several suggestions for fixing this, [9,10,13,16,19,25,27,30,35,36], beginning with the ideas of Rall [30].

An explanation for the failure of (2.9) for problems in more than one variable will motivate the acceleration schemes discussed in this section. If $x_0 \in W(\rho,\theta)$ and x_1 is given by (2.9), there is no reason to expect that $x_1 \in W(\rho,\theta)$. If $x_1 \notin W(\rho,\theta)$ then $F'(x_1)$ may be singular or may have small eigenvalues, x_2 could be far away from the root or not defined at all.

The recent ideas for avoiding this problem are all based on (2.6). We interpret (2.6) as saying that as the iterates progress, they move more and more deeply into $W(\rho,\theta)$, with the X-component becoming much smaller than even the square of the N-component. With this information one can modify the scheme given by (2.9) to force the iterates to remain in $W(\rho,\theta)$. The idea is to take one or more regular Newton iterates between the modified ones.

Two early ways for doing this, [9,16], required the additional assumption that

$$P_N F'''(x^*)(\phi,\phi,\phi) \neq 0 . \tag{2.10}$$

(2.10) is not true, of course, for the H-equation in the form (1.1) or for any other quadratic problem. It is satisfied for the H-equation in form (1.2), however. Both of these approaches start with $x_0 \in W(\rho,\theta)$ and sequences of intermediate iterates. To describe these we let $s(x) = -F'(x)^{-1}F(x)$ denote the Newton step. The method of [9] is

$$
\begin{aligned}
y_n &= x_n + s(x_n) , \\
x_{n+1} &= y_n + (I + P_N)s(y_n) .
\end{aligned}
\tag{2.11}
$$

The method in [16] is

$$
\begin{aligned}
y_n &= x_n + s(x_n) , \\
z_n &= y_n + s(y_n) , \\
x_{n+1} &= z_n + 2s(z_n) .
\end{aligned}
\tag{2.12}
$$

The result is that if all the hypotheses of Theorem B hold, and if (2.10) holds, then the sequences $\{x_n\}$ given by either (2.11) of (2.12) are in $W(\rho,\theta)$ and converge quadratically to x^*.

The method in (2.11) requires computation of a sufficiently accurate approximation to P_N, that in (2.12) requires the computation of an additional Newton iterate. The total cost is about the same. (2.12) has the advantage of being easier to program. Both have the substantial disadvantage of requiring (2.10), which is a condition on the third derivative. The reason for that requirement is to force $\tilde{x}_{n+1}$ to have N-component large enough to be in $W(\rho,\theta)$. If one tries either of (2.11) or (2.12) on the quadratic form of the H-equation, (1.1), the iterates behave erratically, but not as badly as they do if no intermediate iterates are taken.

The elimination the need for assumption (2.10) and a reduction in computational effort is provided by the following scheme, [25],

$$
\begin{aligned}
y_n &= x_n + s(x_n) \\
x_{n+1} &= y_n + (2 - C||s(y_n)||^\alpha)s(y_n) .
\end{aligned}
\tag{2.13}
$$

The idea behind this is that, for $x \in W(\rho,\theta)$, the intermediate iterate would make the X-component of $\tilde{y}_n$ small enough so that

$$||\tilde{y}_n + 2s(y_n)|| = O(||\tilde{x}_n||^2) . \tag{2.13}$$

The remaining term in the expression for x_{n+1} has a sufficiently large N-component to force $x_{n+1} \in W(\rho, \theta)$. The price paid for this is that the iterates no longer converge quadratically. In fact,

$$||\tilde{x}_{n+1}|| = |C|4^{-1-\alpha}||\tilde{x}_n||^{1+\alpha} + \text{higher order terms} . \tag{2.14}$$

We state this as a theorem.

Theorem C: *Let F and* x^* *satisfy the hypotheses of Theorem B. Then for any given* $C \neq 0$ *and* $\alpha \in (0,1)$ *there are* ρ *and* θ *so that if* $x_0 \in W(\rho, \theta)$, *the iterates* $\{x_n\}$ *given by (2.13) converge q-superlinearly to* x^* *with q-order* $1+\alpha$.

The best choice of C and α is problem dependent. One might think, from consideration of (2.14), that one should choose C near 0 and α near 1 to make the error in x_{n+1} small. However, if C is too small or α too large, x_{n+1} may not remain in $W(\rho, \theta)$. We have found that $C = 1$ and $\alpha = .5$ are reasonable choices for many problems.

Recently we have found that the modified Newton iterates given by (2.13) can be improved a bit more. The improvement is based on the iterative method of Shamanskii, [2,29,37], in which a Newton step is followed by a given number, k-1, of iterates with the Jacobian not updated. If we count one iterate as including both the Newton iterate and the subsequent iterates that use the same Fréchet derivative, the convergence rate is superlinear with q-order k+1 for problems with invertable Jacobian at the root. Note that if k=1, Newton's method results.

For singular problems that satisfy the hypotheses of Theorem B, and with k=2, one obtains linear convergence with ratio 3/8. However, one can modify the algorithm in (2.13) by not evaluating $F'(y_n)$ but using $F'(x_n)$ instead. The new approach is

$$y_n = x_n + s(x_n)$$
$$r_n = -F'(x_n)^{-1}F(y_n) \tag{2.15}$$
$$x_{n+1} = y_n + (4 - C||r_n||^{\alpha})r_n .$$

The result here is that if $\alpha \in (0, .5]$ the conclusions of Theorem C hold. An analysis similar to that in [2] indicates that the scheme in (2.15) should be about 20% more efficient than that of (2.13) for problems with large dimension.

2.3. Broyden's Method

When derivative evaluations are expensive, quasi-Newton methods offer superlinear convergence without derivative evaluations for problems with invertable Jacobian at the root. For problems in R^n, the simplest quasi-Newton method is Broyden's method, [3]. Here, from current approximations to the root, x_c, and to the derivative, J_c, new approximations, x_+ and J_+ are computed as follows

$$s = -J_c^{-1}F(x_c) \, ,$$

$$x_+ = x_c + s \, , \text{ and}$$

$$J_+ = J_c + \frac{F(x_+)s^t}{s^t s} \, . \tag{2.16}$$

Broyden's method, when applied to problems with nonsingular Jacobian at the root, will converge superlinearly if x_0 and J_0 are sufficiently near x^* and $F'(x^*)$ respectively, [4,14,15].

For singular problems of the kind considered here, the case of a nonlinear equation in one variable offers insight again. For problems for which $f(x^*) = f'(x^*) = 0 \neq f''(x^*)$ the secant method will converge to x^* at an asymptotically linear rate of $\sqrt{5} - 1/2$. For finite dimensional problems that satisfy the hypotheses of Theorem B, this is the case as well for Broyden's method, [12]. There was no analysis in [12] of equations in infinite dimensional spaces, although we did observe that for $c \leq 1$ the behavior of the iterates for finite dimensional approximations to the H-equation did not change as the dimension became large, exhibiting linear convergence when $c = 1$ and superlinear convergence when $c < 1$.

The formulation of Broyden's method that we used for the H-equation used weighted inner products that, as the dimension became large, approximated the inner product on $L^2[0,1]$. Hence, our Broyden iterates were, in the limit approaching a method whereby J_c is updated by a rank one integral operator, with kernel

$$F(H_c)(\mu)s(\nu)/||s||_{L^2}^2 \, . \tag{2.17}$$

Examples are known, [20,39], of infinite dimensional problems that have only linearly convergent Broyden or other quasi-Newton iterates yet this did not seem to happen with our approximate H-equations and $c < 1$.

Recent results, [20,34], give conditions under which Broyden's method will produce superlinearly convergent iterates in infinite dimensional Hilbert spaces. In addition to all the assumptions required in finite dimensional spaces, the error, $J_0 - F'(x^*)$, must be compact. We have, but not with a microcomputer, observed that for the H-equation, written as (1.2), the iterates approach the superlinearly convergent sequence of the infinite dimensional problem and proved that such is the case for several classes of integral equations.

The observations here began with microcomputer experiments to see how increasing the dimension of an approximating problem to an integral equation changed the convergence behavior. We monitored the ratios of the norms of the steps and found that these ratios seemed to approach a limit as the dimension increased. We were limited to problems of dimension about 100 on the micro. On mainframes one may increase the dimension and observe that this behavior is maintained. Such observations led directly to the results in [26].

REFERENCES

(1) P.B. Bosma and W.A. DeRooij, Efficient methods to calculate Chandrasekhar's H-functions, Scientific Report, Vrije Universiteit Amsterdam, 1983.

(2) R.P. Brent, Some efficient algorithms for solving systems of non-linear equations, SIAM J. Numer. Anal. 10(1973), 327-344.

(3) C.G. Broyden, A class of methods for solving simultaneous equations, Math. Comp., 19(1965), 577-593.

(4) C.G. Broyden, J.E. Dennis, and J.J. Moré, On the local and super-linear convergence of quasi-newton methods, Math. Comp., 12(1973), 223-246.

(5) I.W. Busbridge, The Mathematics of Radiative Transfer, Cambridge Tracts, no. 50, Cambridge Univ. Press, Cambridge, 1960.

(6) K.M. Case and P.F. Zweifel, Linear Transport Theory, Addison Wesley, Reading, Mass., 1967.

(7) S.Chandrasekhar, Radiative Transfer, Dover, New York,1960.

(8) D.W. Decker and C.T. Kelley, Newton's method at singular points I, SIAM J. Numer. Anal., 17(1980),66-70.

(9) D.W. Decker and C.T. Kelley, Convergence acceleration for Newton's method at singular points, SIAM J. Numer. Anal., 19(1982),219-229.

(10) D.W. Decker, H.B. Keller, and C.T. Kelley, Convergence rates for Newton's method at singular points, SIAM J. Numer. Anal., 20(1983), 296-314.

(11) D.W. Decker and C.T. Kelley, Sublinear convergence of the chord method at singular points, Numer. Math.,42(1983),147-154.

(12) D.W. Decker and C.T. Kelley, Broyden's method for a class of problems having singular Jacobian at the root, SIAM J. Numer. Anal., 22 (1985), 566-574.

(13) D.W. Decker and C.T. Kelley, Expanded convergence domains for Newton's method at nearly singular roots, SIAM J. Sci. Stat. Comp., 6(1985), 951-968.

(14) J.E. Dennis and J.J. Moré, A characterization of superlinear convergence and its application to quasi-Newton methods, Math. Comp.,28(1974),549-560.

(15) J.E. Dennis and R.B. Schnabel, Numerical Methods for Nonlinear Equations and Unconstrained Optimization, Prentice-Hall, Englewood Cliffs, N.J., 1983.

(16) A. Griewank, Analysis and modification of Newton's method at singularities, Thesis, Australian National University, 1980.

(17) A. Griewank and M.R. Osborne, Newton's method for singular problems when the dimension of the null space is > 1, SIAM J. Numer. Anal.,18(1981),179-189.

(18) A. Griewank and M.R. Osborne, Analysis of Newton's method at irregular singular points, SIAM. J. Numer. Anal.,20(1983),747-773.

(19) A. Griewank, On solving nonlinear equations with simple singularities or nearly singular solutions, (submitted for publication).

(20) A. Griewank, The superlinear convergence of secant methods on mildly nonlinear problems in Hilbert space, (submitted for publication).

(21) L.V. Kantorovich and G.P. Akilov,Functional Analysis in Normed Spaces, Pergamon, New York, 1964.

(22) H.B. Keller, Geometrically isolated nonisolated solutions and their approximation, SIAM J. Numer. Anal., 18(1981), 822-838.

(23) C.T. Kelley, Solution of the Chandrasekhar H-equation by Newton's method, J. Math. Phys., 21(1980),1625-1628.

(24) C.T. Kelley, Approximate methods for the solution of the Chandrasekhar H-equation, J. Math. Phys., 23(1982), 2097-2100.

(25) C.T. Kelley and R. Suresh, A new acceleration method for Newton's method at singular points, SIAM J. Numer. Anal.,20(1983),1001-1009.

(26) C.T. Kelley and E.W. Sachs, Broyden's method for approximate solution of nonlinear integral equations, J. Int. Eqs., 9 (1985), 25,44.

(27) C.T. Kelley, A Shamanskii-like acceleration scheme for nonlinear equations at singular roots, (submitted to Math. Comp.).

(28) T.W. Mullikin, Some probability distributions for neutron transport in a half space, J. Appl. Prob., 5(1968) ,357-374.

(29) J.M. Ortega and W.C. Rheinbolt, Iterative Solution of Nonlinear Equations in Several Variables, Academic Press, New York, 1970.

(30) L.B. Rall, Convergence of the Newton process to multiple solutions, Numer. Math., 9(1961),23-37.

(31) L.B. Rall, Rates of convergence of newton's method, MRC Technical Summary Report no. 1224, Mathematics Research Center, Madison, WI., 1972.

(32) G.W. Reddien, On Newton's method for singular problems, SIAM J. Numer. Anal., 15(1978),993-996.

(33) G.W. Reddien, Newton's method and high order singularities, Comput. Math. Appl., 5(1980), 79-86.

(34) E. Sachs, Broyden's method in Hilbert space, (to appear in Math. Prog.).

(35) R.B. Schnabel, Conic methods for unconstrained minimization problems and tensor methods for nonlinear equations, University of Colorado Technical Report, Dept. of Computer Science, University of Colorado, Boulder, Colorado, 1982.

(36) R.B. Schnabel and P.D. Frank, Tensor methods for nonlinear equations, SIAM J. Numer. Anal., 21 (1984), 815-843.

(37) V. E. Shamanskii, A modification of Newton's method, Ukran. Mat. Zh., 19 (1967), 133-138.

(38) E. Schroeder, Ueber unendlich viele Algorithmen zur Auflosung der Gleichungen, Math. Ann. 2(1870), 317-365.

(39) J. Stoer, Two examples on the convergence of certain rank-2 minimization methods for quadratic functionals in Hilbert space, Lin. Alg. Appl. 28 (1979), 217-222.

A System for Numerical Linear Algebra

WILLIAM GROPP*

Abstract

Numerical linear algebra plays a significant part of large-scale scientific computing. We describe a system, called CLAM, which provides an environment for researchers to go from pilot studies to quality Fortran programs. By providing a consistent environment from workstation to mainframe, and by providing access to powerful, low cost array processors, CLAM allows the researcher to move smoothly from algorithm development to "real world" problem solving. After describing some of the issues in designing software for interactive, large-scale scientific computing, we illustrate the ideas by presenting some recent work in domain decomposition using a prototype system.

1. Introduction

Small but powerful workstations are becoming available for scientific computing. The amount of computing power that they make available to an individual researcher encourages us to move away from the batch-oriented model of computing and towards a more dynamic interaction between the user and the computer. In Section 2 we describe some basic features which a scientific workstation should have, and distinguish between a personal computer (PC) and the supermicros. We show that the supermicros have fewer restrictions than the PCs and are more suitable for the mathematics researcher. In Section 3, we discuss how a workstation should be used, describing some of the features an environment for scientific computing should provide. In Section 4, we illustrate what can be done on a personal workstation, showing examples of solving elliptic and hyperbolic PDEs with CLAM, a prototype system developed by Scientific Computing Associates, Inc. Finally, an example of using CLAM in current research on domain decomposition methods is provided.

*Yale University, New Haven, Connecticut, 06520, and Scientific Computing Associates, Inc., New Haven, Connecticut, 06510.

This work was supported in part by Office of Naval Research Contract #N00014-82-K-0184, National Science Foundation Grant MCS-8106181, and Air Force Office of Scientific Research Contract AFOSR-84-0360, and in part by Scientific Computing Associates, Inc.

2. The workstation

There are four main areas of concern in a workstation for scientific computing. They are the application software, the compute speed of the workstation, the network and file system, and the "native", vendor supplied software such as the operating system and the display software.

As in the personal computer market, the application software is the most important consideration. A researcher or engineer in scientific computing should spend most of his or her time doing work, not writing software.

In the area of compute speed, workstations fall into two categories: PC's (Personal Computers) such as the Apple and IBM personal computers, and the Supermicros, such as the Apollo, Digital microvax II, and Sun. The PCs are characterized by relatively limited physical memory and even more limited address space, limited secondary (disk) storage, and relatively slow CPUs. Their current advantage is their cost: only a few thousand dollars. The supermicros are small only in size. Current supermicros have nearly unlimited address space (gigabytes), large amounts of physical or main memory (almost 10 megabytes), fast CPUs, comparable to a VAX 11/780, and large amounts of disk space (hundreds of megabytes). Of course, this is more expensive than a PC. However, the cost is far lower than a mainframe, and most of these supermicros do not require any special environment, such as cooling, power, or air filtering.

While there is much that can be done with a PC, there are many limitations which reduce the productivity of people writing or using programs on one, relative to a newer supermicro or, in some cases, mainframes. Principle of these limitations is the limited memory model of the processors used in these PCs. The 64kbyte sections put a severe crimp on any program which must deal with a large amount of data. For example, 64kbytes is only 8192 double precision real numbers, which would just be enough to represent a 90 by 90 mesh of scalars. And while there are tricks which can be used to get past this limitation, they are just that, tricks. These tricks are also less than reliable; many programs including some widely distributed operating systems for PCs still suffer bugs caused by the 64 kbyte section limitation. Most serious is that these tricks aren't applicable on larger, faster computers. Other problems include less helpful error messages. A message like "You may have meant (instead of [here" is more useful than "(?) Syntax error", but requires more of the limited memory in a PC. Smaller working spaces are another problem. In an interactive system, less memory is available to store results which the user is working on. A related problem is the limitation on program size. This restricts the amount of code which may be devoted to solving a problem. For example, in the case of solving linear systems of equations, there is no one best method. For small system, Gaussian elimination is best. As the system gets larger, banded or sparse direct methods become preferable, eventually losing to various iterative techniques. Any program which provides many algorithms will need a large amount of address space simply to hold the machine code for those algorithms. In a supermicro, all of these limitations are either absent or greatly reduced.

Another big advantage of the supermicros over both PCs and larger mainframes is the amount of computing power available to each researcher. The newest supermicros, using the microvax II chip or the 68020 chip, have demonstrated compute power of about that of a VAX 11/780. This is enough power to run significant model problems, but hardly enough to handle "real world" applications, such as 3-D fluid flow or finite element calculations. This points out another consideration for the scientific workstation: the environment used on it should run on larger systems as well.

One other disadvantage of individual workstations is the isolation it creates between workers. The easy sharing of information, the common set of utilities on a mainframe all encourage workers to work together and reduces duplicated effort. To compensate for this lack of community, many workstations provide a network which links the workstations together. The goals here are reliability, performance, and transparency. The least common of these is *transparency*, the ability to operate across a network as if it wasn't even there. In a completely transparent system, a file or program may exist anywhere on the network and be used as if it were local, without any special commands or prefixes. Performance for most networks is adequate, though significant improvements can be expected in the future. Reliability is another problem. Both network hardware and software are still likely to cause problems, though the ethernet hardware seems relatively robust.

Finally, one of the most attractive aspects of workstations are their displays. Such mulitwindow graphics displays provide the user with the ability to work more efficiently, by providing multiple views of the same object (graphics, text file, program) or multiple views of different objects (running program, mail, editing). However, such versatility comes at a price: any software which makes extensive use of such displays is not portable, as no adequate standard has yet emerged. Also, the technology used in bitmap and raster displays is different from the older vector displays, with many basic operations on bitmaps not even supported on many vector displays (e.g., erase line).

3. Making the most of your workstation

A workstation is not just a private computer. It offers new and more productive ways to accomplish tasks. Thus, it is necessary to re-examine how one works when you move to a workstation.

In scientific computing, Fortran has been the language of choice for almost three decades. However, Fortran was designed for a very different environment than that provided by a workstation. The major problem with Fortran is its "Batch" orientation, Typically, a program is written in its entirety and then run. This does not make use of a workstation's ability to provide immediate feedback. Another problem for the scientific computing researcher is the level of detail in Fortran. For most work, the level of detail (variable types, index conventions, declaration of arrays) is unnecessary to the content of the program, and only slows down a researcher. There are also portability difficulties in Fortran. Though Fortran has shown itself to be remarkably portable, there are a number of areas where problems exist. One is in the "processor dependent" parts of the Fortran language. For example, one valid interpretation of `character` variables is that `character` variable may have no more than *one* character. Another is in the "unsafe" nature of the language; the most common manifestation of this is "array out-of-bounds".

The programming environment around Fortran is also a problem. The lack of a common source language debugger makes program development on different systems very time-consuming. And despite the developments in computer graphics standards such as GKS [3], there is in practice no common graphics environment, particularly on window-oriented workstations.

Given these problems, what might we do instead? The Artificial Intelligence (AI) community has long used the so-called *non-procedural* languages. These are basically interactive languages which give immediate response, contain a rich and structure set of operations, and a complete environment including file system, graphics, and debugger. Such a system can also be constructed for scientific computing. An early such system, Matlab [5], achieved great success on mainframes.

However, the needs of a researcher in scientific computing differ both from those in AI and the target of Matlab. These needs can be summarized as

- Functionality
- Speed and size
- Graphics
- Input and output
- Upward compatibility
- Help

In scientific computing, the basic operations might be

- Solve linear systems; perform matrix decompositions
- Basic vector operations
- Solve ODEs numerically, numerical quadrature, non-linear equations

In addition, these operations must apply to large as well as small problems. The actual choice of algorithm used should, at least by default, be made by the system. These operations must be fast enough to handle large problems and general enough to be applicable in a wide range of problems. The algorithms chosen must be robust, accurate, and fast. In many cases, several algorithms will have to be supplied to handle different cases of the same problem (e.g., dense, banded, and sparse matrices).

It is important that any system allow a researcher to investigate large problems as well as small. A system which is only useful for small problems will encourage workers to start in Fortran, since they will eventually have to write Fortran anyway to get any "real" results. In other words, the system must be able to handle more than just toy problems. In many cases, this will imply some form of sparse data structure in order to be able to fit the problem description into main memory. And to be able to solve the problem fast enough, some form of "back-end" processor might be used. An example would be either a mainframe compute server, or a special purpose high speed attached processor. The system would thus provide the researcher with access to special purpose equipment in a transparent, efficient, and portable fashion.

In the area of graphics, the system must provide for quality 2 and 3-D displays, as well as handle multiple devices. As in the case of speed and size, if the graphics capability is not adequate for all tasks, there will be a tendency to ignore it and use a more general purpose graphics program. The graphics should take advantage of the interactive abilities of a workstation, for example allowing a user to use a mouse to control the placement of a label or the size of a graph. One other problem is where the graph is placed relative to the window in which the user input is being typed. Does it go in the same window? Another window? What happens if the program is being used on a "dumb" terminal? All of these questions must be answered based on the capabilities of the workstation and experience of users with actual systems.

Input and output are essential to get large and small data and programs into and out of the system. This must include formatted input and output, since no free-format system can be smart enough to always generate exactly the right amount of data. For portability reasons, the system should provide a uniform means of accessing the workstation's file system, including the creating, editing, and deleteing of files.

And at least as important is the ability to edit data and programs. For example, it should be possible to "edit" a matrix, changing a few entries in it, and then re-entering it. The same should be possible with programs written in the system's language.

The help system should be complete and helpful. This may seem obvious, but few programs or environments meet this goal. Complete means that all commands and actions are described, and that a user has a good chance of finding help even if the command name is not known. This may be done by keyword search or a structured help tree. Further, it should be possible to get quick prompts as well as lengthy help descriptions. For example, at any point in the user's input, it should be possible to display a list of acceptable commands. Finally, the help system should provide just enough help. If the user needs only usage information, then it is not helpful to also generate two pages of detailed description. The reverse is even less helpful. This argues for a tree or list structured help system.

Last, the system should run on a wide range of machines. Fast as any workstation is, there will always be some problem which is too large or long for it. If a program has been developed in some convenient environment on the workstation but must be converted into Fortran in order to be run on a larger compute engine, much of the advantage of the original development will be lost. There may even be a penalty, now that two or more different versions of the same code must be maintained. Thus, the system should run on large mainframes as well as on workstations.

However, there will always be times when Fortran must be generated. On example might be research on ways of solving a particular kind of linear system which arises as part of a much larger code. While even solving the full linear system can be done on the workstation or a compute server, the results of the work will need to be integrated with the original code. This suggests that it be possible to generate Fortran from the programs used in the interactive system.

4. Examples

In this section, we describe a system which fulfills many of the design goals stated above. The purpose of this section is to give one example of what has been done on a workstation (the Vaxstation I) and represents a prototype. This system is called CLAM, for Computational Linear Algebra Machine. Its basic capabilities include the simple arithmetic operations, matrix functions (eigenvalues, norm, matrix division), logical operations, control structures (if—then—else, do—enddo, break, next), user defined, recursive functions, an integral debugger and debugging aids, input and output and a file system interface, and a powerful help system. The primary data object is the matrix; scalars and vectors are handled as special cases. This system has several special features. One is that CLAM maintains matrices in one of several storage formats; the actual format is chosen by CLAM as it sees fit. The decision is in part based on the amount of storage required in each form and the amount of work needed to convert between types. Another feature is that the choice of algorithm to perform a task such as *eigenvalue* is made by CLAM and depends on the data structure and other properties of the matrix. In the case of eigenvalues, the properties checked include real or complex and symmetric or hermitian. In addition, CLAM works hard to insure that both input and run-time errors will be pinpointed.

In the next few sections, we give a few examples to show what can be done quickly in CLAM. We follow that with some current research into domain decomposition methods for solving linear systems arising from the numerical solutions of partial differential equations.

4.1. Help

At any time, CLAM can generate a list of legal input. To get the list, the user types "?", followed immediately by a return. To those familiar with Digital's TOPS-20 operating system, this is similar to command completion, a feature widely appreciated by users of TOPS-20. The list is generated automatically by the table-driven parser, and so is always correct. The lower case names refer to generic objects. "intnum" is any integer, "proc_id" is any procedure name. As a concrete example, here are two uses of this feature:

```
1> ?
#              (              +            -            ;              <
[              ~              BREAK        CLEARPLOT    DEBUG          DECLARE
DELETE         DIARY          DIRECTORY    DO           ECHO           EDIT
end-of-file    EXIT           FREE         HELP         ident          IF
INCLUDE        intnum         LIST         LOAD         LONG           LOOP
NEWS           NEXT           NODIARY      NOECHO       OPTIMIZE       PRINT
proc_id        PROCEDURE      PROCS        QUIT         quoted         realnum
RETURN         SAVE           SHORT        SPACE        UNWATCH        VARS
WATCH          WORKSPACE

2> a = ?
#       (        +        -        ;        <        [        ~        ident
intnum  proc_id quoted   realnum
```

CLAM also contains a complete help system. The HELP command enters a help mode, at the root of a help tree. By moving down the tree, the user gets more and more specific information about CLAM. In addition, the user may ask for all topics that match a search pattern, or for help by keyword list. In the latter case, the user may want to find help on eigenvalues without knowing the appropriate commands. In that case, the user types "like" followed by the keyword. Here is an example: 1> help

```
Information available:

CLAM           Logon-Logoff    Sample-Session IF                       DO
LOOP           BREAK-NEXT      PROCEDURE      INCLUDE                   DIARY
EDIT           VARS            PROCS          PRINT                     FREE
PLOT           SIZE            WATCH          UNWATCH                   DEBUG
LONG/SHORT     ABS             SQRT           LOG                       Trig
NORM           EIG             QR             SVD                       FPS
REAL           IMAG            CONJUGATE      FIX                       FFT
```

IFFT	MAX	MIN	COMPLEX/REAL	Operators
Errors	Miscellaneous	Subscripts	WORKSPACE	LIST
Panic				

```
Topic? like eigenvalues
  1    EIG
Topic? 1
```

The format of the EIG function is
    EIG (mat1)
        or
    EIG (mat1, mat2)

In the first case, only the eigenvalues are returned. In the second case, the eigenvalues are returned as the value of the function and the eigenvectors are stored in mat2.

4.2. Solving an elliptic PDE

With this example, we begin to show how CLAM and a workstation allow a researcher to solve non-trivial problems. This example shows how to numerically solve

$$\nabla^2 u = 0$$
$$u(x, y) = \begin{cases} 0 \text{ if } y = 0 \text{ or } x = 0 \\ 1 \text{ if } y = 1 \text{ or } x = 1 \end{cases}$$

using a simple 5-point difference stencil. The code is shown in Figure 1. The notation a{i,j} refers to the jth element on the ith diagonal, and allows the diagonally structured matrices often encountered in solving PDEs to be constructed easily and clearly. The numerical solution of the PDE is the vector $x = A^{-1}b$, in CLAM this is written as A \B, and the reshape converts the resulting solution vector into a 20 × 20 matrix for plotting. Note that the size of the matrix in this example is 400 × 400, or 160000 matrix elements. Because CLAM takes advantage of the zero structure of the matrix, CLAM can both efficiently store and solve with this matrix.

4.3. Solving a hyperbolic PDE

This section shows how the basic vector operations in CLAM may be used to numerically solve a hyperbolic PDE. We also take advantage of the graphics capability to display the solution as a function of time and space simultaneously. The differential equation is

$$\frac{\partial u}{\partial t} + u\frac{\partial u}{\partial x} = 0$$
$$u(x, 0) = \sin(2\pi x)$$
$$u(0, t) = u(1, t)$$

The program and the results are shown in Figure 2. Note how clearly the graphical output displays the formation of an N-wave, as well as the characteristic oscillations of the Lax-Wendroff method. The decay of the shock is also clearly demonstrated by the

```
procedure formmatrix( n )
a    = 4 * identity( n * n )
! set each row of the matrix.  This approach includes the borders
do i=2:n-1
    s    = [n*(i-1) + 2:n*i - 1]
    a{1,s-ones(1,n-2)}     = -1
    a{-1,s+ones(1,n-2)}    = -1
    a{n,s-n*ones(1,n-2)}   = -1
    a{-n,s+n*ones(1,n-2)} = -1
enddo
return( a )
end

procedure formrhs( n )
b    = zero( n*n, 1 )
! set the rhs.  It is zero except at the borders, where it is
! 4 * bndyvalue
b(1:n)            = 4 * ones(n,1)
b(2*n:n**2-n:n) = 4 * ones(n-2,1)
return( b )
end

a = reshape( formmatrix(20) \ formrhs(20), 20, 20 )
plot( a )
```

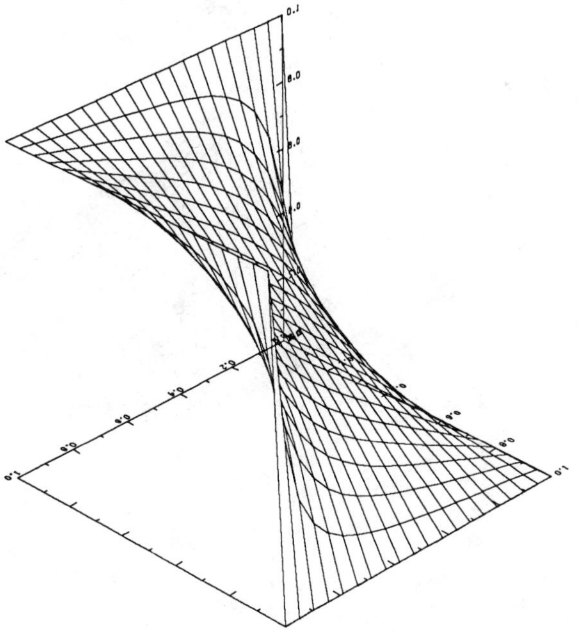

Figure 1: CLAM solving a Laplace Equation.

```
procedure lax2( u, lambda, t, td )
! Integrate u for t steps, saving every td steps.
n         = size(u)(2)
cnt       = ucnt  = 0
l         = .25 * lambda
l2        = l**2
do i=1:t
    urotm  = [ u(n), u(1:n-1) ]
    urotp  = [ u(2:n), u(1) ]
    u      = u - l * (urotp**2 - urotm**2 ) +
               l2 * ( (urotp + u) .* (urotp**2 - u**2) -
                        (u + urotm) .* (u**2 - urotm**2) )
    if ((cnt+=1) >= td) then
        usav(ucnt+=1,*) = u
        cnt                = 0
    endif
enddo
return( usav )
end


h   = 0.02
u   = lax2(u=sin( 2*#pi*h*[0:1/h-1] ), .5, 100, 5)$
plot( u )
```

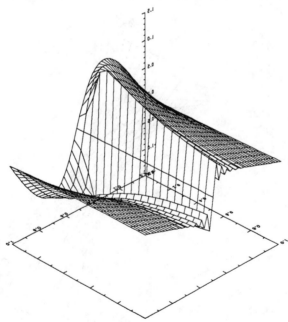

Figure 2: CLAM solving a hyperbolic PDE.

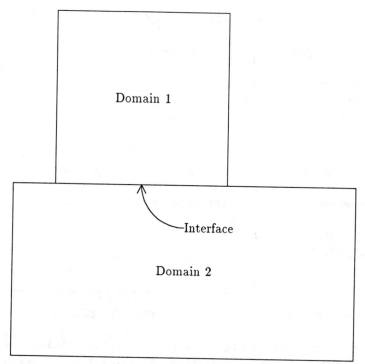

Figure 3: Sample domain. The PDE on this domain is the Poisson equation $\nabla^2 u = f$.

graphical output. This example could have been done on any mainframe. But without an easy way to generate both the data and the graphics, most people would not have bothered. The advantage of a workstation, coupled with powerful software, is that it encourages researchers to find different ways to look at things.

4.4. Domain Decomposition

Our last example is from some current research on domain decomposition methods for solving linear systems of equations. This work is being done with David Keyes of Yale University, and will be reported on at length in [4]. In the domain decomposition method, the domain is divided up into two or more subdomains (c.f. Figure 3). On each of these domains, a conventional fast solver can be applied, either exactly (for Poisson's equation) or as a preconditioner for an iterative method. On a two domain example, we can break the original problem

$$Au = f$$

into

$$\begin{pmatrix} a_{11} & 0 & a_{13} \\ 0 & a_{22} & a_{23} \\ a_{13}^T & a_{23}^T & a_{33} \end{pmatrix} \begin{pmatrix} u_1 \\ u_2 \\ u_3 \end{pmatrix} = \begin{pmatrix} f_1 \\ f_2 \\ f_3 \end{pmatrix}$$

where a_{11} refers to the first domain, a_{22} to the second, and the other terms have to do with the interface between the domains. u_1 is the solution in domain 1, u_2 is the solution in domain 2, and u_3 is the solution along the interface between the domains.

```
procedure precond ( a11, a22, a33, a13, a23, n1, n2, n3 )

! Golub & Mayers' preconditioner for the interfacial unknowns

    aux  = trdiag ( n3, 2 )
    b33  = (aux + 0.25 * aux ** 2) ** 0.5
    return ( b33 )

end
```

```
procedure precond ( a11, a22, a33, a13, a23, n1, n2, n3 )

! Dryja's preconditioning for the interfacial unknowns

    b33  = (trdiag ( n3, 2 )) ** 0.5
    return ( b33 )

end
```

```
procedure precond ( a11, a22, a33, a13, a23, n1, n2, n3 )

! lumped tridiagonal preconditioning for the interfacial unknowns
    aux      = a13' * ( a11 \ (a13*ones(n3,1)) ) +
               a23' * ( a22 \ (a23*ones(n3,1)) )
    b33{0,*} = aux'
    b33      = a33 - b33

    return ( b33 )

end
```

Figure 4: Three different preconditioning routines for solution of (1).

We can use block Gaussian elimination to reduce this to a problem on the interface equations alone:

$$Cu_3 \equiv (a_{33} - a_{13}^T a_{11}^{-1} a_{13} - a_{23}^T a_{22}^{-1} a_{23}) u_3 = f_3 - a_{13}^T a_{11}^{-1} f_1 - a_{23}^T a_{22}^{-1} f_2. \qquad (1)$$

Once this is solved for u_3, we can get u_1 and u_2 from

$$u_1 = a_{11}^{-1} (f_1 - a_{13} u_3)$$
$$u_2 = a_{22}^{-1} (f_2 - a_{23} u_3).$$

The principle difficulty here is in forming the C matrix in Equation 1. While it is expensive to compute C directly, it is much less expensive to compute Cv, where v is an arbitrary vector. This suggests using the Conjugate Gradient method to solve for u_3. And since it is well know that the Conjugate Gradient method is far more effective when preconditioned, we need to look at what kind of preconditioners should be used.

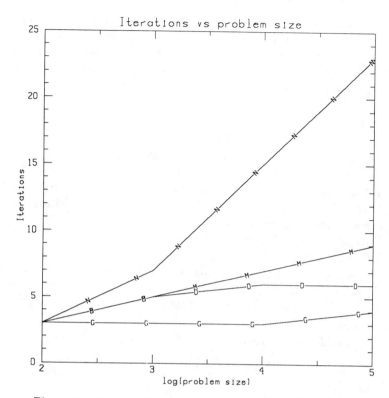

Figure 5: Results of tests of preconditioners for domain decomposition. The data for log(problem size) = 5 involved solving a linear system with roughly 3000 unknowns.

A number have been proposed, and the example we present here compares them on the domain in Figure 3. To test these preconditioners, we wrote a preconditioned conjugate gradient routine in CLAM which calls a routine to perform the preconditioning. The preconditioning routines are shown in Figure 4. Using these preconditioners with our CLAM PCG program, we quickly obtain the graph shown in Figure 5.

This graph shows the iteration count as a function of problem size. The line labeled N is non-preconditioned conjugate gradient. M is the lumped tridiagonal preconditioning [4], D is the Dryja preconditioning [1], and G is the Golub-Mayers preconditioning [2]. It took far less time to program and compute these results in CLAM than it would in Fortran.

5. Conclusion

In conclusion we see that the current generation of scientific workstations now puts a tremendous amount of power in the hands of the researcher. Workstations with large amounts of real, virtual, and secondary memory, fast CPUs, and high resolution (1024 × 1024, not just 300 × 600) graphics allow significant model problems to be solved. But to get the most of these advantages, we must move away from the batch, Fortran oriented approach used on mainframes. Further, the rapid developments in workstation hardware argue strongly against developing systems which must deal with the limitations of the last generation of hardware, such as memory addressing limitations. We have presented a series of requirements and objectives for such a computing environ-ment, considering both the hardware and the software, and demonstrated its feasibility with an actual prototype system. The next few years should see tremendous gains in the productivity of applied mathematics researchers who take advantage of these new capabilities.

References

[1] M. Dryja, *A Capacitance Matrix Method for Dirichlet Problem on Polygonal Region*, Numer. Math., 39 (1982), pp. 51–64.

[2] G. H. Golub and D. Mayers, *The Use of Pre-Conditioning over Irregular Regions*, 1983.   Lecture at Sixth Int. Conf. on Computing Methods in Applied Sciences and Engineering, Versailles, Dec. 1983.

[3] F. R. A. Hopgood et al., *Introduction to the Graphical Kernal System (GKS)*, Academic Press, 1983.

[4] D. E. Keyes and W. D. Gropp, *A comparison of domain decomposition techniques for elliptic partial differential equations and their parallel implementation*, 1985.   To appear as a Yale Department of Computer Science Research Report.

[5] C. Moler, *MATLAB Users' Guide*, 1981.

Modeling with Ray-Tracing
in 2-D Curved Homogeneous Layered Media

V. PEREYRA*

Abstract: Algorithms for ray-tracing in a piecewise homogeneous medium with curved layer interfaces are described. Normal incidence and non-zero offset two-point and shooting are considered. Travel time and amplitude calculations are used in the generation of synthetic seismograms. Also, time-to-depth migration of seismic sections, an inverse problem, is described. The whole package has been implemented in a microcomputer, and it is integrated into a complete modeling system to aid the interpreter of seismic reflection surveys.

1. Introduction

A ray-tracing based modeling package has been developed for a micro-computer environment. In this paper we will discuss the theoretical and practical details of its implementation on an IBM-PC-XT machine. The purpose of the development was to provide an existing system, the Geological Modeling System (GMS) of Kim Tech Inc., Denver, Colorado, with a more powerful and versatile ray-tracing module. The original plan has been extended to cover some aspects of automatic inverse modeling, such as time-to-depth migration of material interfaces.

The types of media considered consist of piecewise constant velocity layers separated by curved interfaces. Pinchouts and other nonconformities are allowed in order to be able to model complex regions with interesting geological features.

The ray-tracing system is source-receiver oriented; i.e. with a two-point or global philosophy, although shooting is used to provide automatic starting and re-starting after failure capabilities. The two-point approach, coupled with appropriate continuation procedures, is considerably more efficient than conventional

* Weidlinger Associates, Palo Alto, CA 94304.

shooting-trapping techniques [1,9,10]. Parameterization in reflector offset or initial angle is used in order to make the algorithm robust and so that multiple arrivals can be obtained.

In the current implementation we have chosen to consider generalized curved layer media in order to cope with pinchouts, terminating layers, and the like. By generalized layers we mean layers that run across the whole model window, but that can be locally thin (i.e. pseudolayers). This approach simplifies noticeably the logic necessary for describing and tracing rays, since no checking is necessary when a layer disappears at a pinchout, etc.; however, it limits the generality of models that can be treated, and it will be changed in the future to one based upon connectivity information.

The interactive features already present in the menu-driven GMS allow the digitized input of models, easy input of material properties, and postprocessing of ray-traced time-amplitude data in the form of synthetic seismograms. With the addition of the ray-tracing capabilities, this provides a very versatile work station for performing many, if not all, of the most important tasks needed in the forward and, in a limited sense, inverse modeling of reflection data, in a user-friendly manner.

At present the system has options for normal incidence and non-zero offset ray-tracing. Both primary, secondary and tertiary reflections, to any or all the interfaces of the model can be requested. Also diffractions from pinchout corners can be generated. For each ray, geometrical spreading and elastic reflection-transmission coefficients are calculated. In the case of diffracted arrivals, the exact solution for the diffraction of a plane wave by a wedge [7] is used to generate the amplitude. Finally, successive time-to-depth migration of selected digitized horizons can be effected via ray-tracing, both for post- and pre-stack time sections.

The system and the hardware (especially if an IBM-AT machine with a floating-point co-processor is used) are sufficiently fast as to make this otherwise arithmetic hungry task a plausible proposition in an interactive environment. It goes without saying that these capabilities are considerably enhanced by the ease by which graphics can be integrated into the system.

2.   Basic Algorithm for Two-Point Ray-Tracing

We consider two-dimensional piecewise homogeneous media separated by curved interfaces. To begin, we assume that the interfaces are non-intersecting, smooth, one-valued curves:

$$z = f_i(x) \ , \ i=1,\ldots,Last \quad , \quad x \in [x_m, x_M].$$

These conditions will be relaxed later on. Figure 1 depicts a typical model of this type.

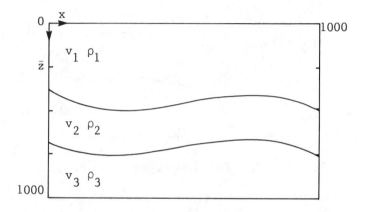

Figure 1.   Typical layered model.

A geological window is chosen, and a Cartesian (x,z) system of coordinates is laid on it, with z (depth) running positive downwards. Interfaces are numbered consecutively downwards, the free surface being #1. The layers are numbered in a similar fashion, and v_i, ρ_i are, respectively, the velocity of propagation and density for layer i. Velocity can be either that corresponding to pressure or shear waves.

In Fig. 2 we see pictorially the two-point, ray-tracing problem: Given a source S and a receiver R, we want to find the ray (or rays) that join S and R, after traversing through or reflecting from a specified sequence of interfaces.

In conventional reflection surveys, both sources and receivers are usually on the free surface. However, in vertical seismic profiling, receivers, and sometimes sources, will be down a borehole, so it is of interest to consider the more general case of source and receivers in arbitrary locations.

The sequence of interfaces and regions a ray tra-
verses is called its <u>signature</u>. Signatures are given in
two integer arrays (ICR,IRG), whose lengths are related
to the number of legs of the ray. Thus, in the example
of Fig. 2, the depicted ray has signature:

$$ICR = [2,3,2,3,2,1] \quad , \quad IRG = [1,2,2,2,2,1]$$

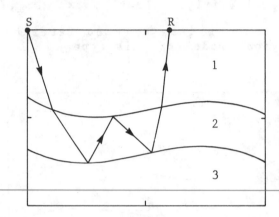

Figure 2.   Two-point ray-tracing.

Rays are defined as paths of minimum (actually sta-
tionary) time, through which a point disturbance travels
from S to R. In the present case, it is well-known that
these paths are straight segments that break at interfaces, where the velocity of propagation varies discon-
tinuously.   The break in direction of the rays is gov-
erned by Snell's law of geometrical optics.

Let $\underset{\sim}{\nu}$ be the normal to the interface at the point of
contact with the ray, and let ϕ^-, ϕ^+ be the angles that
the incoming and outgoing ray segments form with $\underset{\sim}{\nu}$.
Snell's law says that

$$v^+ \sin \phi^- = v^- \sin \phi^+ \tag{1}$$

Thus the mathematical problem of calculating a ray
joining a source-receiver pair, with a given signature,
is reduced to finding the intersections of the cross-
ings, so that Snell's law is satisfied. In the general
case of curved interfaces, this will give a coupled
system of nonlinear equations. A very clean version of
the resulting system of equations has been given in
H. B. Keller and D. J. Perozzi [6].

The first observation is that we can reduce the
problem even further to just finding the offsets of the

intersections, since we can use the equations of the interfaces to calculate the depths.

Let $X = (x_0, x_1, \ldots, x_{N+1})$ be the sequence of offsets defining the ray, where $x_0 = x_S$, $x_{N+1} = x_R$. According to the signature $ICR(j)$, the corresponding depths will be

$$z_j = f_{ICR(j)}(x_j) \quad, \quad j=1,\ldots,N \quad. \tag{2}$$

A tangent to interface $ICR(j)$ at x_j is given by

$$\tau_j = (1, f'_{ICR(j)}(x_j))^T$$

and Snell's law (1), can be expressed by means of vector inner products as :

$$\psi_j(X) = v_{IRG(j+1)} <\tau_j, r_j> - \tag{3}$$
$$v_{IRG(j)} <\tau_j, r_{j+1} >= 0 \quad,$$
$$j=1,\ldots,N$$

where (r_j) $j=1,\ldots,N$ represent normalized ray directions; i.e. if

$$\underset{\sim j}{w} = \begin{pmatrix} x_j \\ z_j \end{pmatrix} - \begin{pmatrix} x_{j-1} \\ z_{j-1} \end{pmatrix}$$

then $r_j = w_j / |w_j|$, where

$$|w_j|^2 = (x_j - x_{j-1})^2 + (z_j - z_{j-1})^2 \quad,$$

and z_j is given by (2).

The travel time between source and receiver is easily obtained as

$$T_{SR} = \sum_{j=1}^{N+1} |r_j| / v_{IRG(j)}$$

The set (3) of N nonlinear simultaneous algebraic equations must be solved in order to find the unknown offsets $x_1, \ldots, x_N$. In vector form, (3) is represented as $\underset{\sim}{\psi}(X) = 0$.

The method of choice for finding solutions to such systems is Newton's method. Given an initial guess $\mathbf{x}^0$, we compute corrections by means of the iteration: For i=0,... :

Solve the linear system of equations

$$A(\mathbf{x}^i) \; \delta\mathbf{x}^i = - \underset{\sim}{\psi}(\mathbf{x}^i) \tag{4}$$

where $A(\mathbf{X}) = \delta\psi / \delta\underset{\sim}{\mathbf{X}}$ is the Jacobian matrix of the system.

$$\text{Correct:} \quad \mathbf{x}^{i+1} = \mathbf{x}^i + \delta\mathbf{x}^i. \tag{5}$$

The matrix $A(\mathbf{X})$ is tridiagonal, since only three unknowns are coupled in each equation, and therefore the solution of the linear systems can be achieved in order N^2 operations.

Sometimes Newton's method has difficulties in converging; for instance, if the initial values do not belong to the domain of attraction of the desired solution. A way to prevent divergence in the early stages, or on difficult regions, is to take only a fraction of the Newton step $\delta\mathbf{x}^i$. The rationale for this strategy is that the Newton iteration is of descent for the functional $|\underset{\sim}{\psi}(\mathbf{X})|$, and therefore, if we take $t > 0$ sufficiently small

$$|\underset{\sim}{\psi}(\mathbf{X} + t\delta\mathbf{X})| < | \underset{\sim}{\psi}(\mathbf{X})|.$$

Initially, we would try to use the full Newton step, i.e. $t=1$, but if the norm of the residual increases with respect to the previous iteration, then t will be diminished. Since failure or difficult convergence may be an indication that no solution exists (i.e. shadow zone), we do not let our Newton search wander too much. That is also where our very effective restarting procedure comes into play.

A usual task is to calculate a whole family of rays with the same signature. Once a first ray has been successfully obtained, a natural continuation procedure is to use this ray to estimate a starting trajectory for the next one in the family. Euler continuation is proposed for this purpose in [2,6]. Using the difference of two consecutive previous rays works as well and it is considerably cheaper; thus we use Euler continuation only to start our second ray. Once this has been successfully calculated, we switch to the more economical procedure.

Either type of continuation will give erroneous starting guesses when we get close to a fold in the wave front, as in the buried focuses produced by synclines (see Fig. 3), and that will make Newton's method fail.

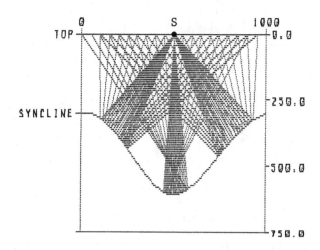

Figure 3.   Triplications due to syncline.

Thus, in the presence of multiple solutions, as in the triple coverage shown above, simple continuation in receiver offset will fail to produce all the arrivals. The reason for this failure is intimately connected to continuation and the bifurcation of branches of solutions of nonlinear equations depending on parameters [5].

The problem we are considering can be stated more precisely as that of solving a family of nonlinear equations $\psi(\mathbf{X}, x_R) = 0$, parameterized by receiver offset.

If we plot the time $T(x_R)$ that the signal takes to travel from source to receiver, we soon realize that the familiar travel time curves (as function of offset) are also the bifurcation diagrams for this nonlinear problem (see Fig. 4, where the travel time curves are given as synthetic seismograms).

The bifurcations in this case correspond to the corners of the bowtie. A simple offset continuation procedure will follow one of the branches, namely, the one in which its initial ray lays, until it comes to the end of the branch at one of the turning points or goes off the window. Only by accident will the Euler continuation make it jump to another branch. Elaborated procedures for navigating through turning and bifurcation points are available [5,12,13], but we have preferred to take a different tack, as explained below.

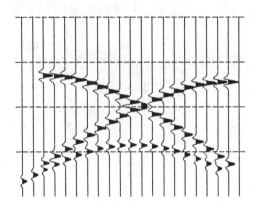

Figure 4.   Travel time curves as synthetic seismograms.

What we mentioned above is just one type of possible failure of Newton's method. A robust algorithm that wants to compute as many arrivals of a given type as possible must have provisions for restarting, and also for avoiding the re-calculation of already computed rays. The way in which we have been able to solve all these problems in an unified way is to parameterize the search with respect to the initial ray angle ϕ_0. Clearly, there is a one-to-one mapping between these angles and the corresponding rays, since a given initial position and initial direction determines uniquely a ray of a given signature.

We do not give up receiver continuation, which is a useful procedure within continuous, slowly varying branches of solutions, but we supplement it with a careful bookkeeping of the initial angles searched. Start and restart after failure is provided via shooting and (fairly loose) trapping. To describe the procedure in more detail and to fix ideas, let us consider the case of a source on the free surface.

Let $[\phi_L, \phi_R] \subset [-\pi/2, \pi/2]$ be the interval of possible initial angles that will generate all the rays of the given signature, starting from S and reaching a family of evenly spaced receivers, also assumed to be on the free surface. Such an aperture can be estimated at the outset, or in the worst of cases the whole interval $[-\pi/2, \pi/2]$ can be considered.

This angle interval is then searched in a systematic fashion starting, say, from ϕ_L. The first ray is shot with this angle, and if it reaches the free surface within the receiver window, then an appropriate modified version is used to start the two-point scheme for a ray from the source to the closest receiver. If the two-pointing is successful, we record the computed initial angle, and any gaps in angle larger than a given threshold are also saved in a stack, as angle subintervals to be searched later for possible additional arrivals.

The goal of the algorithm is to make sure that within a given maximum resolution, i.e. a minimum angle gap $\Delta\phi$, the whole angle aperture is checked for possible ray solutions. Apparently this same objective could be achieved by shooting systematically $(\phi_R - \phi_L)/\Delta\phi$ rays, and picking those that land within a prescribed tolerance from a receiver. However, examination shows that the sensitivity of arrival offset with respect to initial angle can be made arbitrarily high, which will in turn require a very small $\Delta\phi$ in order for this alternative procedure to be successful. The main advantage of two-pointing and receiver continuation is that a much more economical procedure results, since the gap in ϕ corresponding to two consecutive receivers need not be checked for further arrivals, regardless of its size.

The algorithm is recursive, insofar as the stack of angle subintervals to be revised varies dynamically, and the process ends when this stack is empty, meaning that the whole initial search interval has been visited, within the given resolution. Whenever a multiple arrival is computed, its initial angle and travel time are compared with those of previous arrivals to the same station (and of the same family, in case multiple families are being considered simultaneously), and if a close match occurs, then the new arrival is declared a repetition and it is disregarded.

3. Basic Algorithm for Shooting Rays

The shooting of rays through layered structures, such as those considered earlier, still requires equation solving to obtain the intersection of ray segments with the curved interfaces. With the same notation as in Section 2, the problem to be considered here is to shoot a ray from a given source position S (x_0, y_0), with a given initial angle ϕ_0, through a curved layered structure, according to the signature given in the arrays ICR, IRG (see Fig. 5).

Let $S_i = \begin{pmatrix} x_i \\ z_i \end{pmatrix}$, i=1, ..., N+1, be the unknown

intersections with the interfaces. The straight line segment that starts at S_i, with direction ϕ_i is parameterized as

$$L_i (\lambda) = S_i + \lambda P_i , \lambda > 0 ,$$

where

$$P_i = \begin{pmatrix} \sin\phi_i \\ \cos\phi_i \end{pmatrix}, \quad L_i(\lambda) = \begin{pmatrix} L_{ix}(\lambda) \\ L_{iz}(\lambda) \end{pmatrix} .$$

For each leg i, we want to solve the scalar nonlinear equation

$$\rho(\lambda) = L_{iz}(\lambda) - f_{ICR(i+1)}(L_{ix}(\lambda)) = 0 \qquad (6)$$

for $\hat{\lambda}_i$. Then $S_{i+1} = L_i(\hat{\lambda}_i)$.

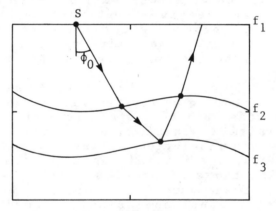

Figure 5.   Shooting a ray.

We could use Newton's method to solve these scalar equations, but a more robust, and usually just as efficient, procedure is ZEROIN [3], a combination of bisection, the chord method and cubic extrapolation. We have enhanced the standard algorithm by adding a search to ensure that the interval in λ given to ZEROIN is such that the function $\rho(\lambda)$ changes sign at the end points, as required but not enforced by the original code. Another reason for preferring this algorithm instead of a Newton type one, is that in the way we have implemented it, no initial guesses are necessary, and except for very extreme geometries, an initial interval with a change of sign is rapidly found. After that

ZEROIN guarantees the return of a root with the desired accuracy.

Once an intersection S_{i+1} is found, Snell's law provides a mean to obtain the direction P_{i+1} of the next leg of the ray. In fact, we have that if

$$\underset{\sim}{\tau}_i = (1, \; f'_{ICR(i)} \; (L_{ix} \; (\hat{\lambda}_i)))/(1+f'^2_{ICR(i)})^{1/2}$$

and $v_i = v_{IREG(i)}$, then P_i and P_{i+1} must satisfy

$$\bar{v}_{i+1} < \underset{\sim}{\tau}_i, \; P_i > \; = \; \bar{v}_i < \underset{\sim}{\tau}_i, \; P_{i+1} >. \tag{7}$$

Since $\underset{\sim}{\tau}_i, \; P_i, \; P_{i+1}$ are co-planar, we must have

$$P_i = P_{i+1} + \beta \; \underset{\sim}{\tau}_i$$

for some scalar β. Taking inner product with $\underset{\sim}{\tau}_i$, we get

$$< \underset{\sim}{\tau}_i, \; P_i > \; = \; < \underset{\sim}{\tau}_i, \; P_{i+1} > \; + \; \beta \; ,$$

or

$$\beta = [\; < \underset{\sim}{\tau}_i, \; P_i > \; - < \underset{\sim}{\tau}_i, \; P_{i+1} > \;] \; ,$$

and replacing the value of $< \underset{\sim}{\tau}_i, \; P_i >$ from (7), we get

$$\beta = [\bar{v}_i/\bar{v}_{i+1} - 1 \;] < \underset{\sim}{\tau}_i, \; P_{i+1} > \quad .$$

Therefore, the new normalized direction P_{i+1} is:

$$P_{i+1} = (P_i - \beta \; \underset{\sim}{\tau}_i) \; / \; | \; P_i - \beta \; \underset{\sim}{\tau}_i \; | \; ,$$

and we can go back to (6), with i increased by 1. The algorithm terminates when P_{N+1} and the corresponding last intersection S_{N+1} are generated.

This type of shooting algorithm provides an automatic way of starting the two-point solver for the first time and also, through the use of our search stack, to restart it upon failure. This may occur in the neighborhood of a folding of the travel time curve, or when the rays get close to abrupt changes in the interface geometry or material properties.

4. Normal Incidence Ray-Tracing

Various types of processing are performed on measured seismic reflection data in order to improve its quality and simultaneously reduce the volume of data that has to be manipulated.

One of these processes consists of taking the signal corresponding to a coincident source-receiver pair, and adding to it those of nearby receivers, with appropriate time corrections. This process is referred to as _stacking_, and if performed and displayed for every source, it produces a normal incidence or stacked section.

The name normal incidence stems from the fact that the only way for a ray to go from a point on the free surface, bounce in a deep horizon (say #L), and return to the same point following the same path, is that the angle of incidence with horizon L be 90 degrees (see Fig. 6). Of course, with complex curved layers it is possible to have nonnormal incident rays with zero-offset, but those will only be considered as special cases of our non-zero offset calculations.

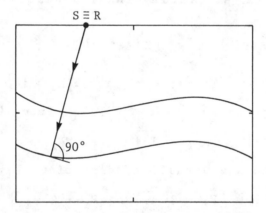

S ≡ R

90°

Figure 6.   Normal incidence ray-tracing.

The algorithms for both two-point and shooting normally incident rays are just small modifications of the ones for the general problem. Of course, since the path to the deep horizon coincides with the return path, only half of the work needs to be done. For two-pointing, equations (3) are set for all the interfaces up to the L-1 and, as the last equation we add the normal incidence condition

$$< \underset{\sim}{\tau}_L \, , \, r_L > \, = 0 \, . \tag{8}$$

Travel time will be recorded as the two-way travel time.

The type of shooting that we will be interested in doing requires that the ray start normally from an arbitrary point on the deep reflector, and travel   to the free surface, say, with the given signature. This type of ray will provide good starting guesses for the normal incidence two-point calculation.

Also this points out to the correct parameterization to ensure complete coverage of all possible arrivals. Namely, we will use offset along the deep reflector as the search parameter, just as we used initial ray angle at the source for non-zero offset bookkeeping. Clearly, provided that the deep reflector is a one-to-one function of x, this will give a one-to-one correspondence between the parameter space and all the possible normal incidence arrivals. Therefore, it is an adequate parameterization for continuation through travel time curve foldings, as opposite to simple receiver offset.

Again, the normal incidence shooting algorithm is similar to the one we described in Section 3 for the non-zero offset case. The only two differences are:

a)   The ray is traced from a point (x_0, y_0) on the deep horizon L to the free surface (say).

b)   The initial angle is predetermined as

$$\phi_0 = \cos^{-1}(\underset{\sim}{\tau}_L) \quad,$$

where $\underset{\sim}{\tau}_L$ is the normalized tangent vector to interface L at x_0.

Just as in the case of non-zero offset, this procedure does not require starting guesses, and therefore is ideally suited to provide starting and restarting rays for the two-point process. A stack of unsearched subintervals of deep reflector offsets is kept, and the search ends only when this stack is empty. The only additional care we take is to scale the search step, to take into account the interface slope. If $z=f(x)$ is the equation for the interface, we scale the basic search step x , that measures the attainable resolution, as

$$\tilde{\Delta}x = \Delta x / \text{sqrt}(1 + (f')^2) \quad.$$

So, the steeper the interface the smaller will be the actual search step. This amounts to an arc-length based equidistribution of the density of points that will be examined.

5.   Pinchouts and Other Nonconformities

As promised, in this section we explain how to handle pinchouts, and some apparently multivalued interfaces, like those necessary to model reverse faults.   A

pinchout occurs when a layer evanesces within our geological window, as shown in Fig. 7.

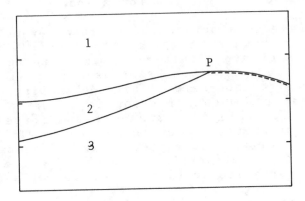

Figure 7.   A pinched-out layer.

Curved, or even straight, but dipping interfaces
imply lateral variations of velocity, which cause problems in many of the standard geophysical data processes.
Pinchouts provide even more extreme examples of those
types of difficulties, and additionally, pinchout tips
produce diffracted arrivals that complicate the picture
even further.

To be able to include this and other nonconforming
situations, we follow and idea of Cerveny et al. [1],
where the introduction of fictitious thin layer segments
is suggested. Thus, we would convert the truncated layer
2 in Fig. 7 into a complete layer, by extending interface 3 parallel to I_2, from the pinchout tip P to the
right end of the model window. In doing this, we actually create a thin layer of non-zero width, which will
essentially be transparent to all the ray-tracing algorithms (and the user). We also keep enough information
about the original, unmodified model, so as to know if
an interface used to be shorter, and thus effect the
correct processing in a number of situations that require special care.   Thus, for all practical purposes,
we are back in the full length case. Multiple pinchouts
are treated in a similar form, and the actual extension
of the layers is done automatically in a preprocessing
step.

A more challenging situation arises when we want to
make a model of a reverse fault, as shown in Fig. 8.   A
somewhat artificial solution to the problem of converting the model of Fig. 8 to a complete layer model is
indicated in Fig. 9.   We have numbered interfaces and

regions in the usual way, used (P_i, Q_i) to indicate the end points of the original segments, and R_2, R_5 to indicate the end points of the added segments.

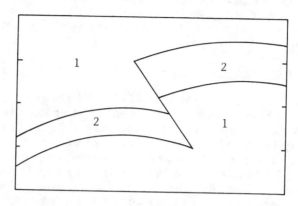

Figure 8.   Reverse fault.

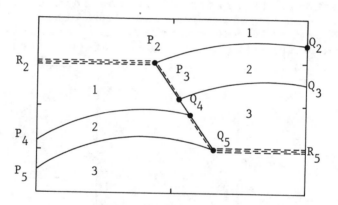

Figure 9.   Layered form of reverse fault.

In short, we complete interface 2 $[P_2, Q_2]$ to the left, with the straight line segment $[R_2, P_2]$, and we take as new interfaces

$$I_3 = [R_2, P_2, P_3, Q_3] ;$$

$$I_4 = [P_3, Q_4, Q_5, R_5] ;$$

$$I_5 = [P_4, Q_4, Q_5, R_5] ;$$

$$I_6 = [P_5, Q_5, R_5] .$$

Of course, in deeper interfaces, parallel segments get displaced by a small amount. The addition of segments $[R_2, P_2]$, $[Q_5, R_5]$, and the judicious input of the actual model segments in the order and form indicated above, will make it look like a collection of pinchouts that can then be converted automatically to a regular layered media as before.

6. Amplitude Calculation

Together with ray paths and travel times, we can also obtain from geometrical ray theory, amplitudes, polarities and phases, which are good high frequency approximations. This amplitude, considered as a peak amplitude, is used to scale a given wavelet, chosen by the user, and placed at the time of arrival in order to generate so-called synthetic seismograms (see Fig. 10). These are time histories recorded at the various stations that try to mimick the way in which the actual collected data is presented in the form of time sections. They provide a visual, qualitative way of matching computed and recorded time histories, thus proving or disproving the adequacy of our model.

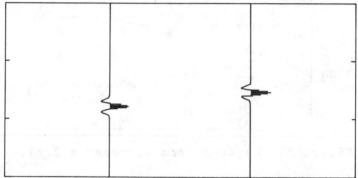

Figure 10.   Part of a synthetic seismogram showing one arrival at two stations.

Once a ray connecting a source and a receiver has been obtained, we compute two different contributions to peak amplitudes: geometrical spreading and reflection-transmission coefficients. The first contribution quantifies the natural spread of energy with distance, and also the geometrical focusing and de-focusing of ray beams due to the curved interfaces. A good formulation of the geometrical spreading calculation for our type of models can be found in Section 3.6 of Cerveny et al. [1]. The second contribution comes from the partition of energy at interfaces. When a ray intersects a material discontinuity, four other rays can be generated: one reflected and one transmitted of the same type, and also reflected and transmitted converted rays (P to S or vice versa).   This partition of energy depends upon the angle of incidence of the ray and the values of velocities and densities on each side of the interface. For the given ray signature, a reflection-transmission coefficient and a phase are generated according to the general formulation of Zoeppritz, as implemented by Young and Braile [11].

The product of the two contributions, the phase and the arrival time are then used to generate a wavelet in the seismogram corresponding to the receiver. Multiple arrivals to the same receiver will appear as additional wavelets, which may interfere with each other to give more complicated wave forms if the arrival times are close together.

7. Diffractions

Interface discontinuities produce a different kind of phenomenon called <u>diffraction</u>. When a wave front intersects an interface at a discontinuity, like a pinchout corner or a break in direction, a diffracted wave front is produced. Because of the discontinuity, standard Snell's law is not valid at such points, and the type of rays we have discussed so far cannot be continued. In 1958, J. B. Keller [8] published a theory that permits to extend the use of rays to this more general situation.

The first point to make is that a ray impinging on a corner or point discontinuity reflects energy in all directions (see Fig. 11). Amplitudes in this case are calculated by considering local, exact solutions to the wave equation for given geometries.

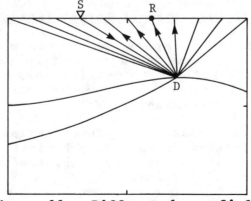

Figure 11.   Diffracted ray field.

The data for computing a diffracted ray-path is, as
usual, the source and receiver positions, the ray signature and additionally the diffractor position. If the
source and receiver are coincident (zero offset), then
the problem is a two-point one, with one end point at
the source receiver location, and the other at the
diffractor. In this case there is nothing new.

Amplitudes are computed in the usual way except at
the diffractor. For the diffracted amplitude field at
pinchout corners, we have implemented the exact solution
for diffraction by a wedge given by J. Keller and Blank
[7]. Of course, the wedges considered there are made of
straight lines, so we use the interface tangents at the
diffractor as an approximation.

In Fig. 12 we show a synthetic seismogram corresponding to the diffractor of Fig. 11.

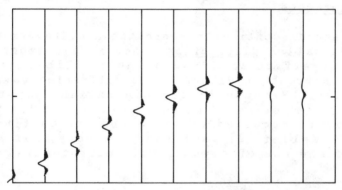

Figure 12.   Synthetic seismograms for diffractors.

For the non-zero offset diffractions we solve two
independent two-point problems, one for the downgoing
[S,D], and one for the upgoing path [D,R], respectively.

8.   Time-to-Depth Migration of Normal Incidence Data

A first step in achieving one of the main goals of
inverse modeling of the Earth subsurface is to convert
time section data into depth section images. Assuming
that the material properties are known, we can describe
this process in our terminology as:

> Given a time versus offset curve corresponding
> to the reflections from a deep horizon, find
> the position of the horizon, i.e. produce a
> depth versus offset image.

This process is called time-to-depth migration.

Travel time curves are picked from recorded sections collected in the field. This is a primary task of the interpreter of seismic reflection data. If the raw data is utilized, then the arrivals will correspond to non-zero offset reflections. Usually, raw data is too noisy for direct interpretation. In order to improve its quality, data processing is performed, producing a stacked section. This type of section simulates a set of normal incidence data.

Unfortunately, stacking often assumes physical condi-tions that are not valid, like horizontal stratifi-cation. Thus, in the presence of lateral variations, as those produced by dipping or generally curved inter-faces, stacking introduces errors (distorting the infor-mation contained in the data) and then migration, after stacking does not produce correct results [4,9].

Naturally, normal incidence sections can be obtained from the original data by just taking the arrivals to the geophones that coincide with the source, or stacking can be limited to only a few nearby receivers. In any case, the inverse modeling of such sections, even if it produces incorrect results, may serve to point defects in the processing, which can in turn be corrected.

The depth migration that we will describe assumes the knowledge of all the velocities and horizons above the desired reflector, and also that a time curve associated with the reflector can be picked from the data. Let this time curve be $T(x_0)$, where x_0 is receiver offset and, for the time being, let us assume that it is single valued and differentiable. Multiple valued, or discon-tinuous time curves will be handled in terms of their single valued smooth segments.

If $P(s) = (x(s), z(s))$ represents the ray path, then

$$d\ T\ (x_0)/dx_0 = \sin \phi_0 / v(x_0) \ , \qquad (9)$$

where ϕ_0 is the ray angle at x_0 measured with respect to the z axes. Therefore,

$$\phi_0 = \sin^{-1} [v\ (x_0)\ d\ T\ (x_0)/dx_0] \ , \qquad (10)$$

and from the measured time curve, we can infer the value of the initial angle ϕ_0. Thus all we need to do is shoot a ray, with initial angle ϕ_0 through the structure, and stop when the time $T(x_0)/2$ has elapsed. At that moment we will have hit the reflector and, if we consider the normal to the ray, then we have both a point and the tangent to the interface.

Of course, real data contains errors and time curves will only be available at a finite number of points, the actual receiver locations. Thus, both $d\,T(x_0)/dx_0$ and $T\,(x_0)$ itself will only be known approximately. For instance, $d\,T\,(x_0)/dx_0$ can be approximated by differences, or a spline can be passed through the discrete data set and the derivative taken as that of the spline. In either case an interpolation error will occur, which will be more or less severe, depending upon the form of the travel time curve. Thus, travel time curves with rapidly varying curvature will tend to produce larger errors than slowly varying ones.

A different question is how errors in the initial angle propagate through the structure or, in other words, how stable is the position of the end point of the shot ray with respect to variations in the initial angle. Actually, the geometrical spreading is a measure of that sensibility, since it quantifies how much an infinitesimal ray tube will spread when propagated through the structure. Thus we can use geometrical spreading to weight the information produced by our computed rays. These weights can be used **a posteriori** in the least-squares generation of an analytic representation of the interface, say by cubic splines or other appropriate parameterization.

Notice that diffracted arrivals should be properly collapsed to a point, this being one of the standard measures of a migrated section's quality. In Figs. 13 and 14 we show synthetic data and its recovery via the above procedure.

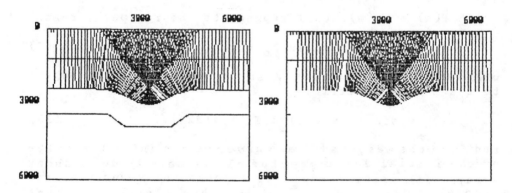

Figure 13.   Synthetic migrated data.

The process will work its way from the free surface down, and therefore horizons will be migrated in succession. If a good velocity model is not known, then additional procedures (not considered in this paper) can be invoked to improve velocities and other material properties, simultaneously or alternating with the migration process.

Finally, in Fig. 15 we show a more ellaborated model, in which some overshooting is apparent when recovering a highly curved piece of horizon.

9. Migration of Non-Zero Offset Data

As we described before, non-zero offset data corresponds to noncoincident source-receiver pairs. Outside of this, the problem is the same as for normal incidence data, although its solution is somewhat more complicated.

Again, from the picked travel time curve $T(x_0)$ we can calculate the ray angle ϕ_0 upon arrival to the station located at $(x_0,0)$. However, shooting backward from $(x_0,0)$ with angle ϕ_0 beyond the last known interface will only provide half of the desired path, since the path from the deep reflector to the source will now be different. In any case, shooting backward from the receiver will produce a unique direction ψ_R from interface $L-1$ downwards (see Fig. 16).

At this point we do not know where the break point P, where the ray should bounce back from the unknown horizon, is located. What we do know is the total travel time that is available for the trip from S to R.

Our solution to the problem consists of shooting with initial angle ϕ_S from S; after traveling through the known structure and traversing horizon $L-1$, another direction ψ_S will be produced. It is then a simple matter to calculate the intersection of the two directions ψ_R, ψ_S: if this intersection occurs in the half space below horizon, $L-1$, then it will be an acceptable candidate for P.

Obviously, we can also compute the time $T^C(x_0; \phi_S)$ necessary to travel from S to R following this path:

if $T^C(x_0; \phi_S) = T(x_0)$ then we are finished.

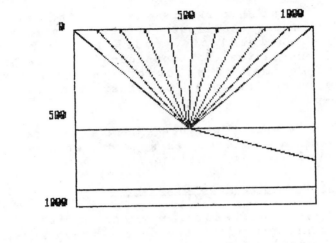

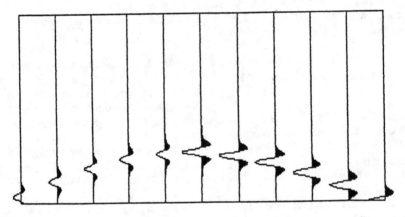

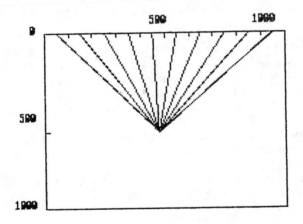

Figure 14.   Synthetic and migrated diffracted data.

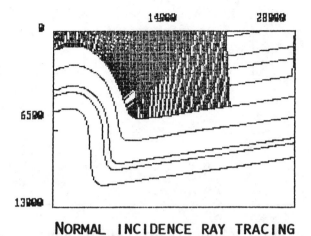

NORMAL INCIDENCE RAY TRACING

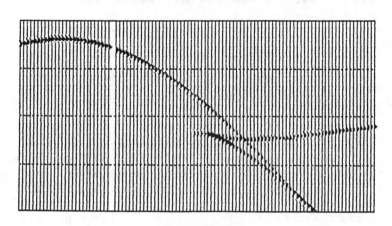

SYNTHETICS

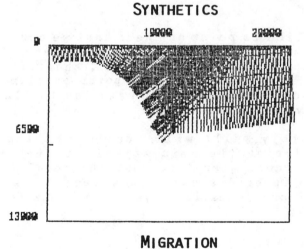

MIGRATION

Figure 15.   Migration of normal incidence data.

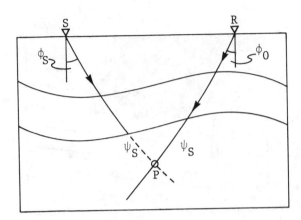

Figure 16.   Schematic migration procedure.

Thus our problem has been reduced to solving the scalar equation

$$T^c (x_0;\ \phi_s) - T (x_0) = 0\ ,\qquad\qquad (11)$$

as a function of ϕ_s, which can be acomplished with a further judicious use of ZEROIN.

In Figs. 17 and 18 we show an example of the application of this procedure using three different sources and a set of 60 receivers for the same model and interface of Fig. 13, where normal incidence was used.   We see some discrepancies, but we must also recall that with non-zero offset data there will be considerable redundancy.

We would like to point out here that we could as well have set up a "two-point problem" to migrate this data. In fact, keeping the first part, i.e. shooting from the receiver, we can formulate a two-point problem from the source to the unknown point P, using as the last equation the travel time matching (11).

Unfortunately, (11) will couple all the points, apparently losing the main appeal of the two-point formulation, namely the fact that the resulting system of equations is tridiagonal. However, if we consider the matrix of our linearized system in block form

$$\begin{pmatrix} T & \underset{\sim}{u} \\ \underset{\sim}{v} & \alpha \end{pmatrix}$$

we see that we can solve the system with two bidiagonal back-solves and a few additional operations.

We have chosen the shooting approach for expediency, since it is simpler and the scalar equation solver is very robust but, of course, the curse of ill-conditioning looms in the background.

10. Comments on Microcomputer Implementation

The description of the system contained in Sections 2 through 9 makes very little reference to the computer environment in which it was developed. This in itself tells some of the story, since the system could as well have been developed on a minicomputer or a mainframe, and only a few years back that would have been the only choice available.

What was different? What influence did the micro-computer environment have in the development and in the actual performance of the system? What characteristics are especially valuable in this environment? In this section we will try to answer these questions based on our current experience.

Since we were adding to an existing system, we had initial constraints that may not be present in other projects. Besides the obvious constraint of communica-tion between the existing and new modules, the main other issue was the fact that GMS was written in BASIC. When this project was initiated there were no other good quality compilers available, that would have allowed us to do as much as we did with BASIC. As with everything else, that has changed considerably in a short period of time. As a consequence, the whole system is now being translated into C. BASIC has obvious disadvantages for developing large systems, mainly its lack of real sub-routines and the global nature of its variables. How-ever, on a PC it has also a number of advantages, noti-ceably: the graphic and string instructions, the inter-preted mode, and the possibility to access extended memory.

The principal concept that comes across in evaluating the system is that it constitutes an <u>economical</u>, self-contained, personal work station for nontrivial geophys-ical modeling that can be used in a production mode for rapid, interactive work, or for training future inter-preters and wave analyzers.

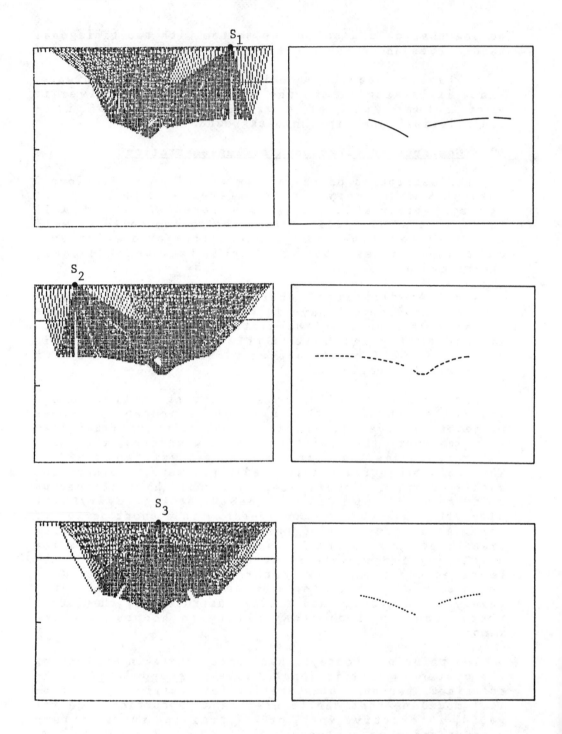

Figure 17.   Recovery of a synclinal from non-zero offset
data (3 sources).

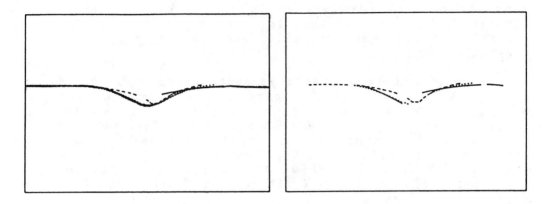

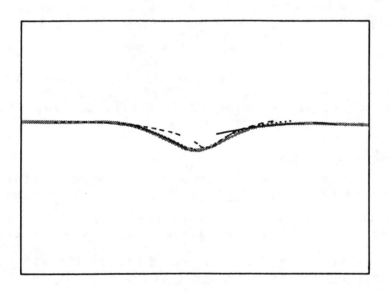

Figure 18. Comparison of exact and recovered horizon.

When the basic configuration (say an IBM-AT) is enhanced with a digitizing tablet, good quality printer,
maybe a high resolution color monitor for graphics, a

separate monitor for interactive input-output, and a floating-point co-processor, it puts at your finger tips a fairly powerful and versatile machine <u>that runs at constant speed</u>.

Obviously, there will always be tasks that go beyond the capabilities of a PC, but then a communication package is all one needs to connect it to the world. For instance, we have developed a three-dimensional ray tracing code for complex media that would not (as yet) transport gracefully to a PC. However, we plan to do a good deal of our interactive 3-D modeling on a PC, and then shift files back and forth, and initiate tasks from it in our mainframe.c

It is important to point out that this is all standard equipment, both hard and soft, that can be purchased from your neighborhood computer store, and therefore is available to the public at large. With more specialized, expensive, and/or experimental equipment, much more can be done right now. But, it will still take some time for these devices to become generally available.

Acknowledgment: This work benefitted from many conversations with my colleague, G. Wojcik. His help and early work in the calculation of diffracted amplitudes is especially appreciated.

References

[1]   V. CERVENY, I. A. MOLOTKOV and I. PSENCIK (1977), <u>Ray Method in Seismology</u>, Univ. Karlova, Praha.

[2]   P. DOCHERTY (1985), "A fast ray tracing routine for laterally inhomogeneous media," Manuscript.

[3]   G. FORSYTHE, M. MALCOLM and C. MOLER (1977), <u>Computer Methods for Mathematical Computations</u>, Prentice Hall, Englewood Cliff, NJ.

[4]   L. HATTON, K. L. LARNER and B. S. GIBSON (1981), "Migration of seismic data from inhomogeneous media," <u>Geophysics</u> 46.

[5]   H. B. KELLER (1978), "Global homotopies and Newton methods," <u>Recent Advances in Numerical Analysis</u> (Ed. C. de Boor and G. H. Golub), Academic Press, NY.

[6]   H. B. KELLER and D. J. PEROZZI (1983), "Fast
      seismic ray tracing," _SIAM J. Appl. Math._ _43_,
      pp. 981-992.

[7]   J. B. KELLER and A. A. BLANK (1951), "Diffraction
      and reflection of pulses by wedges and corners,"
      Comm. Pure Appl. Math. _4_, pp. 75-94.

[8]   J. B. KELLER (1958), "A geometric theory of
      diffraction," _Calculus of Variations and its_
      Applications, Mc Graw Hill, NY, pp. 27-52.

[9]   K. L. LARNER, L. HATTON, B. S. GIBSON and I-C. HSU
      (1981), "Depth migration of imaged time sections,"
      Geophysics _46_, pp. 734-750.

[10] B. T. MAY and J. D. COVEY (1981), "An inverse ray
      method for computing geologic structures from seis-
      mic reflections--Zero offset case," _Geophysics_
      _46_, pp. 268-287.

[11] G. B. YOUNG and L. W. BRAILE (1976), "A computer
      program for the application of Zoeppritz's ampli-
      tude equations and Knott's energy equations," _Bull._
      Seism. Soc. America _66_, pp. 1881-1885.

[12] E. J. DOEDEL and J. P. KERNEVEZ (1985), "Software
      for continuation problems in ODE's with applica-
      tions," to appear in _SIAM J. Sci. & Stat. Comp._

[13] R. SEYDEL (1983), "BIFPACK--A program package for
      calculating bifurcations," Buffalo, NY.

A Singular Perturbation Problem on Microcomputers

GEORGE C. HSIAO* AND PETER B. MONK*

Abstract

   An initial-boundary value problem of a linear parabolic equation
with a small parameter is employed as a model problem to implement
numerical methods for singular perturbation problems on the microcomputer. A modified Crank-Nicholson scheme is developed based on the
asymptotic analysis of singular perturbation theory. Numerical results
are included from both standard and modified schemes. It seems that
by making use of the modified scheme, numerical experiments may be
performed on the microcomputers as effectively as on the large, mainframe computers.

   1. Introduction. In recent years, it appears that use of the microcomputer as a significant tool for scientific computing is increasing
its feasibility, because of the advanced capabilities of microcomputers. In fact, convenience and availability make it preferable to
use the microcomputer over the large mainframe computer. The purpose
of this paper is to explore the possibility for implementing numerical
methods for singular perturbation problems on microcomputers. It
is well known that due to the presence of boundary layers, standard
numerical schemes without modifications are not suitable in general
for the singular perturbation problems even on the mainframe. Through-
out the paper, we shall confine ourself only to the simplest model
problem for the convection dominated diffusion equation.

   For definiteness, we consider here the initial-boundary value problem (P) consisting of the one-dimensional linear parabolic equation

$$\frac{\partial u}{\partial t} + a \frac{\partial u}{\partial x} = \varepsilon \frac{\partial^2 u}{\partial x^2} , \quad 0 < x < 1 , \quad t > 0 \tag{E}$$

together with the initial condition

$$u(x,0) = u_0(x) , \quad 0 \le x \le 1 \tag{I}$$

and the Dirichlet boundary conditions

*Department of Mathematical Sciences, University of Delaware, Newark,
 Delaware 19716

$$u(0,t) = g_1(t) \; , \quad u(1,t) = g_2(t) \; , \quad t > 0 \; . \tag{B}$$

In the formulation, $\varepsilon > 0$ is a small parameter, a is a constant, and without loss of generality we assume that $a > 0$. The given data u_0, g_1 and g_2 are smooth functions satisfying necessary compatability conditions. We are interested in the numerical approximation to the classical solution of the problem for ε sufficiently small.

As is well known, the problem (P) defined by (E) (I) (B) is <u>singular</u> in the sense that the reduced equation

$$\frac{\partial U}{\partial t} + a \frac{\partial U}{\partial x} = 0 \; , \quad 0 < x < 1 \; , \quad t > 0 \; , \tag{E_0}$$

which is a first-order hyperbolic equation, does not possess a solution satisfying both boundary conditions in (B). For $a > 0$, it can be shown that there is a boundary-layer in the neighborhood of $x = 1$ with a thickness of $O(\varepsilon)$. In fact, the exact solution u of (P) admits the asymptotic expansion [1]

$$u(x,t;\varepsilon) = U(x,t) + V(\tilde{x},t) + O(\varepsilon^{1/2}) \quad \text{as} \quad \varepsilon \to 0^+ \tag{1.1}$$

uniformly on $[0,1] \times [0,T]$ for any finite $T > 0$. Here

$$U(x,t): = \begin{cases} u_0(x-at) \; , & x - at > 0 \\ g_1(at-x) \; , & x - at < 0 \end{cases} \tag{1.2}$$

is the reduced solution of (E_0) and V is the boundary-layer solution,

$$V(\tilde{x},t): = \{g_2(t) - U(1,t)\} \, e^{-a\tilde{x}} \tag{1.3}$$

with $\tilde{x}: = (1-x)/\varepsilon$ being the stretched variable. Clearly, the boundary-layer solution V is significant only in the boundary layer where $1 - x = O(\varepsilon)$. It is in this region where one usually has difficulty to obtain an effective algorithm for the numerical approximation to the exact solution. Nevertheless, as will be seen, a good approximation can be achieved even on the microcomputer by modifying the standard numerical scheme according to the asymptotic behavior of the exact solution.

2. <u>The Fourier Solution</u>. In the following, for simplicity, we shall refer to the approximation

$$\tilde{u}: = U + V \tag{2.1}$$

as the <u>singular perturbation solution</u> of the problem (P) where U and V are defined by (1.2) and (1.3), respectively. In order to have some idea about the computational capability of the microcomputer, we simply compute u and $\tilde{u}$ for various small ε. To this end we consider the problem (P) with homogeneous boundary conditions in which case (P) can be solved explicitly by the method of separation of variables. A standard computation shows that the exact solution is then reduced to an infinite series form. We refer to the corresponding truncated series, u_N as the <u>Fourier solution</u> of the problem (P), where N is the total number of terms after truncation. For the special case when the initial function is given by

$$u_o(x) = \sin \pi x , \qquad (2.2)$$

the Fourier solution of (P) is of the form

$$u_N(x,t;\varepsilon): = \{ \sum_{n=1}^{N} b_n e^{-\varepsilon n^2 \pi^2 t} \sin n\pi x \} e^{\frac{a}{2\varepsilon}(x-at/2)} , \qquad (2.3)$$

where

$$b_n: = \frac{32a \, n\pi^2 \varepsilon^3 (1+(-1)^n e^{-a/2\varepsilon})}{(a^2+4(n+1)^2 \pi^2 \varepsilon^2)(a^2+4(n-1)^2 \pi^2 \varepsilon^2)} .$$

We note that roughly speaking, $b_n = 0\left(\dfrac{1}{n^3 \varepsilon} \right)$ and hence more terms need to be computed for smaller ε in order to achieve the same degree of accuracy.

In Figures 1 to 3, we present some of the typical results. All the computations are done by using a straightforward BASIC language program on the IBM PC (and Zenith z100). The curves are plotted by the Epson FX-80 dot matrix printer. It is seen that the Fourier solution

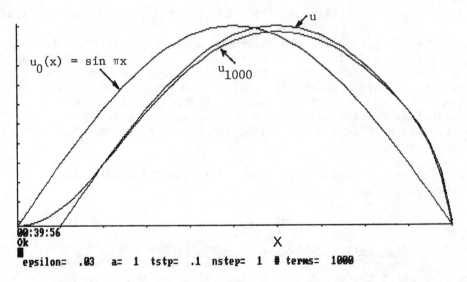

Figure 1. $\tilde{u}$ vs u_{1000} for $t = 0.1(\varepsilon=0.03)$.

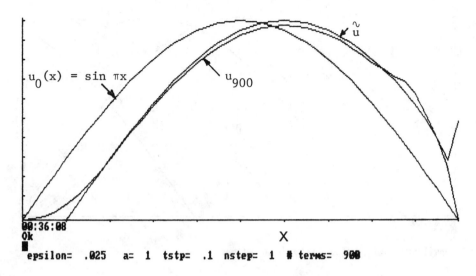

Figure 2. $\tilde{u}$ vs u_{900} for $t = 0.1(\varepsilon=0.025)$

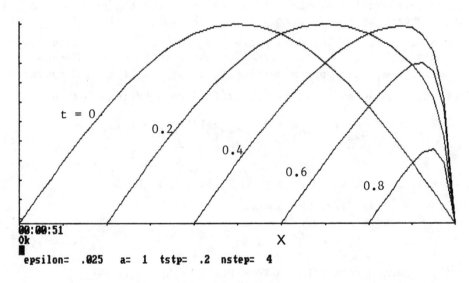

Figure 3. $\tilde{u}$ for various $t(\varepsilon=0.025)$

for small ε will become numerically instable in the boundary-layer for large N (even in double precision). On the other hand, the singular perturbation solutions are relatively stable in spite of very small ε, and do not require much computational time as well. We emphasize that in all the computations so far we have not taken advantage of the presence of 8087 Math Coprocessor.

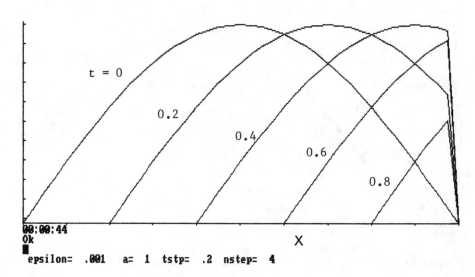

Figure 4. $\tilde{u}$ for various t ($\varepsilon=0.001$)

3. <u>The Crank-Nicholson Scheme.</u> We now apply the standard Crank-Nicholson scheme for treating initial-boundary value problem to the singular perturbation problem (P). We introduce the grid points (x_j, t_n) where $x_j = j\Delta x$ for $j = 0, 1, 2, \ldots, N + 1$ and $t_n = n\Delta t$ for $n = 0, 1, \ldots$. The mesh sizes Δx and Δt are selected such that $\Delta x = 1/(N+1)$ and $\Delta t = 1/M$ for positive integers M and N. We denote by u_j^n the approximation of u at (x_j, t_n) and replace differential equation (E) by the difference equations for u_j^n,

$$\frac{u_j^{n+1} - u_j^n}{\Delta t} + a \frac{u_{j+1}^{n+1/2} - u_{j-1}^{n+1/2}}{2\Delta t} = \varepsilon \frac{u_{j-1}^{n+1/2} - 2u_j^{n+1/2} + u_{j-1}^{n+1/2}}{(\Delta x)^2} \quad (3.1)$$

for $j = 1, 2, \ldots, N$, and $n = 0, 1, 2, \ldots$. Here $u_k^{n+1/2} := (u_k^{n+1} + u_k^n)/2$. Moreover, if we let

$$\lambda := \frac{\varepsilon \Delta t}{2\Delta x^2} \quad \text{and} \quad \mu := \frac{\Delta t}{4\Delta x} \quad (3.2)$$

then (3.1) can be rewritten in the form

$$(1+2\lambda) u_j^{n+1} + (\mu-\lambda) u_{j+1}^{n+1} - (\mu+\lambda) u_{j-1}^{n+1} = \delta_j^n \quad (3.3)$$

for $j = 1, 2, \ldots, N$ and $n = 0, 1, 2, \ldots$, with

$$\delta_j^n := (1-2\lambda) u_j^n - (\mu-\lambda) u_{j+1}^n + (\mu+\lambda) u_{j-1}^n .$$

In principle, this tridiagonal system is ready to be solved by the method of factorization, provided ε is not too small.

Indeed, from (3.3), it is not difficult to see that the following
stability condition (with respect to the sup–norm)

$$\frac{\Delta t}{\Delta x} \leq \frac{\Delta x}{\varepsilon} \leq 2 \tag{3.4}$$

must be fulfilled for (3.3) being stable. This means that we must
choose the mesh sizes to have the same order of magnitude as ε. Hence
the standard Crank–Nicholson scheme is not suitable in practice for
$0 < \varepsilon \ll 1$.

In the following, we include some of the computational results obtained by the standard Crank–Nicholson scheme (3.3). All computations
are in double precision and are done on a Zenith z100 Microcomputer
with 8087 coprocessor by using Microsoft FORTRAN V3.2. The curves
presented here are all plotted by a HP7470 graphics plotter. Figure 5
shows a typical family of the approximate solution curves for various t.

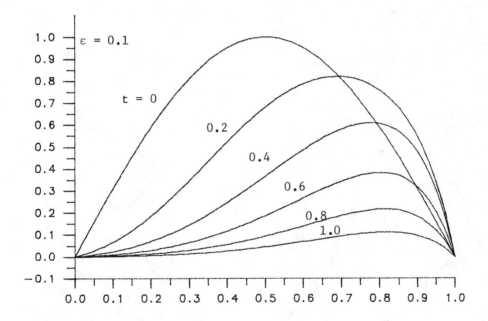

Figure 5. Approximate solution by the standard
Crank–Nicholson scheme with
$\Delta x = \Delta t = 0.01$.

In this case ε (=0.1) is rather large and no boundary–layer appears
in the neighborhood of x = 1. In Figure 6, similar curves are plotted
where the mesh sizes satisfy the stability condition (3.4). However,
the condition (3.4) is not satisfied in Figure 7, and hence small
instability may be noticed at the upper right–hand corner.

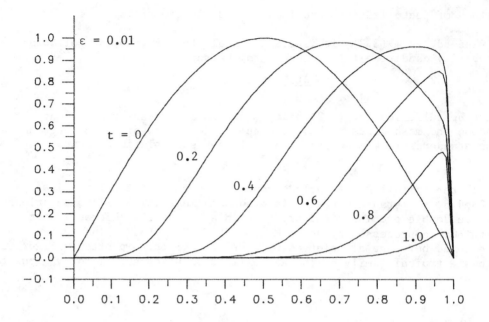

Figure 6.   Approximate solution by the standard
            Crank–Nicholson scheme with
            $\Delta x = \Delta t = 0.01$.

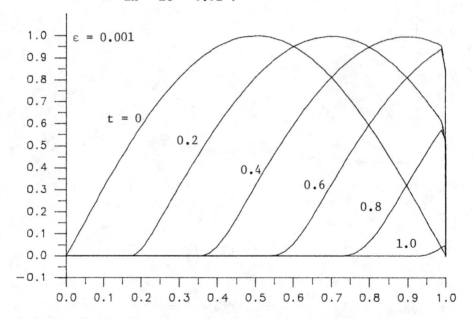

Figure 7.   Approximate solution by the standard
            Crank–Nicholson scheme with
            $\Delta x = 0.001$ and $\Delta t = 0.01$.

For comparison, a list of the computing time required for approximate solutions with various mesh sizes is given in Table 1, in the case $\varepsilon = 0.1$ when there will be no boundary-layer at $x = 1$.

$\Delta x = 1/(N+1)$, $\Delta t = 1/N$		$\Delta x = 1/(N+1)$, $\Delta t = 0.01$	
N	Computing time	N	Computing time
10	1.90 sec	10^2	1.90 sec
10^2	12.81 sec	10^3	1 min 51.19 sec
10^3	16 min 59.22 sec	1.8×10^3	3 min 18.46 sec

Table 1.   Computing time for the approximate solutions by the standard Crank-Nicholson scheme ($\varepsilon=0.1$).

4.   A modified Crank-Nicholson scheme. We modify the standard Crank-Nicholson scheme so that it will be appropriate for singular perturbation problems for very small ε. The essential idea involved here is to replace the Crank-Nicholson equation (3.3) at the last nodal point, x_N by one which takes into account the boundary-layer behavior of the exact solution, but to keep equations at other nodes unchanged. More precisely, let us first take one small interval, close to the right end point $x = 1$, with the mesh width

$$h_\varepsilon := \gamma \varepsilon . \qquad (4.1)$$

Here γ is a factor to be chosen large enough so that h_ε contains the boundary-layer. Next, by introducing the $N - 1$ nodal points, $x_0, x_1, \ldots, x_{N-1}$, we divide the remaining interval $[0, 1 - h_\varepsilon]$ into $N - 1$ sub-intervals with a uniform mesh width h. Our modified Crank-Nicholson scheme then consists of solving the equations in (3.3) for $j = 1, 2, \ldots, N - 1$ and $n = 0, 1, 2, \ldots$, together with the equations,

$$a_N u_N^{n+1} + c_N u_{N-1}^{n+1} = \delta_N^n , \qquad n = 0, 1, 2, \ldots, \qquad (4.2)$$

where

$$a_N := \frac{\Delta x}{\Delta t}\left[\frac{1}{3} + \mu + \lambda\right] + \frac{1}{\Delta t}\alpha_\varepsilon + \frac{1}{2}\beta_\varepsilon ,$$

$$c_N := \frac{\Delta x}{\Delta t}\left[\frac{1}{6} - \mu - \lambda\right] ,$$

and

$$\delta_N^n := \left\{\frac{\Delta x}{\Delta t}(\frac{1}{3} - \mu - \lambda) + \frac{1}{\Delta t}\alpha_\varepsilon - \frac{1}{2}\beta_\varepsilon\right\} u_N^n$$
$$+ \left\{\frac{\Delta x}{\Delta t}(\frac{1}{6} + \mu + \lambda)\right\} u_{N-1}^n$$

with

$$\alpha_\varepsilon := \frac{h_\varepsilon + \frac{\varepsilon}{2}(1-e^{-2h_\varepsilon/\varepsilon}) - 2\varepsilon(1-e^{-h_\varepsilon/\varepsilon})}{(1-e^{-h_\varepsilon/\varepsilon})^2} \tag{4.3}$$

and

$$\beta_\varepsilon := e^{-h_\varepsilon/\varepsilon}(1-e^{-h_\varepsilon/\varepsilon})^{-1} .$$

This modified scheme is, of course, motivatived from the asymptotic analysis in (1.1) - (1.3). In the following, we shall indicate how the equations (4.2) and (4.3) are derived.

First, let us introduce the function $\Phi_\varepsilon: [0,1] \to \mathbb{R}$ defined by

$$\Phi_\varepsilon(x) := \begin{cases} \{1 - e^{-(1-x)/\varepsilon}\}\{1 - e^{-h_\varepsilon/\varepsilon}\}^{-1}, & x \in [1 - h_\varepsilon, 1] , \\ (x-x_{N-1}) h^{-1}, & x_{N-1} \le x \le x_N , \\ 0 , & \text{otherwise.} \end{cases} \tag{4.4}$$

We note that $\Phi_\varepsilon(x) = 1$ at $x = 1 - h_\varepsilon$ and belongs to the Sobolev space $\overset{\circ}{H}{}^1(0,1)$. By following the usual Galerkin finite element approach, we consider the approximation,

$$u^h(x,t_n) = \sum_{j=1}^{N-1} u_j^n \phi_j(x) + u_N^n \Phi_\varepsilon(x) ,$$

where the ϕ_j's, $j = 1, 2, \ldots, N - 1$, are the standard piecewise linear element basis functions [2]. Here the coefficients u_j^n, $j = 1, 2, \ldots, N - 1$ satisfy the algebraic system (3.3) for $j = 1, 2, \ldots, N - 1$ and $n = 0, 1, 2, \ldots$, while the coefficient u_N^n will be determined by the variational formulation of (E) with $a = 1$. That is, we require u_N^n to satisfy the weak equation

$$\frac{1}{\Delta t}(u^h(\cdot,t_{n+1}) - u^h(\cdot,t_n) , \Phi_\varepsilon) + (u_x^h(\cdot,t_{n+1/2}), \Phi_\varepsilon)$$
$$+ \varepsilon(u_x^h(\cdot,t_{n+1/2}), \Phi_\varepsilon') = 0 , \tag{4.5}$$

where $(\cdot,\cdot)$ denotes the L_2-inner product. A simple computation then shows that (4.5) is identical to (4.2). It should be understood that in this formulation, the same initial condition

$$u_j^0 := u_0(x_j) , \quad j = 0, 1, 2, \ldots, N + 1$$

is assumed as in the standard Crank-Nicholson scheme (3.3).

We remark that for $j = 1, 2, \ldots, N - 1$ and $n = 0, 1, 2, \ldots$,
the equations

$$\frac{1}{\Delta t} (u^h(\cdot, t_{n+1}) - u^h(\cdot, t_n), \phi_j) + (u^h_x(\cdot, t_{n+ 1/2}), \phi_j)$$

$$+ \varepsilon(u^h_x(\cdot, t_{n+ 1/2}), \phi_j) \qquad (4.6)$$

$$= 0$$

are not exactly the same as (3.3). However, if $u \in c^2 [0,1]$, it is
not difficult to see that (3.3) and (4.6) are equivalent up to
$O(h^2)$. In this way our scheme, (4.2) and (4.3) may be considered as
a modified Crank–Nicholson Galerkin scheme. The choice of the nonlinear basis function ϕ_ε of (4.4) seems quite natural in view of the
shapes of those curves in Figures 3 and 4.

To conclude this paper we now present some results from our modified
scheme. The curves in Figure 8 computed by the modified scheme are

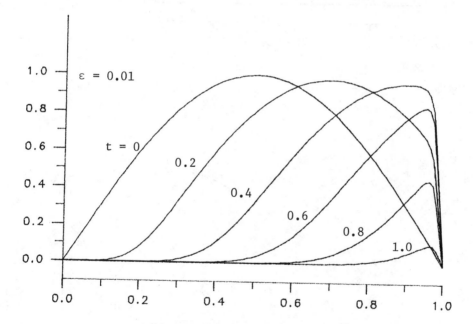

Figure 8.   Approximate solution by the modified
Crank–Nicholson scheme with $\Delta x = \Delta t = 0.01$.

apparently smoother than those in Figure 6 by the standard Crank–
Nicholson scheme. Here we set the factor $\gamma = 1$ in (4.1). In both
figures 9 and 10, we set $\gamma = 5$ and there appears small instability
close to $x = 1$ which may be due to γ too small, while small instability around $u = 0$ results from the fact that the initial data

$u_0(x) = \sin \pi x$ is not smooth enough. Indeed, as can be seen from Figure 11, we have taken the initial data $u_0(x) = 2x \sin \pi x$ and set $\gamma = 10$. Here we have obtained smooth curves for ε as small as 10^{-15}.

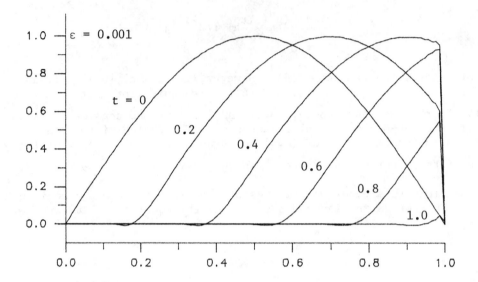

Figure 9.   Approximate solution by the modified Crank–Nicholson scheme with $\Delta x = \Delta t = 0.01$.

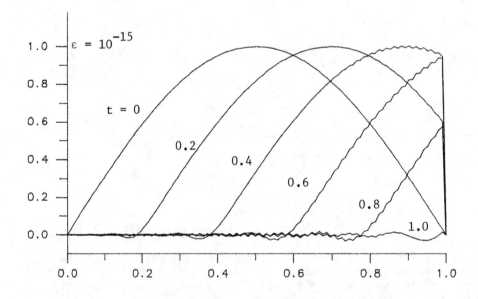

Figure 10.   Approximate solution by the modified Crank–Nicholson scheme with $\Delta x = \Delta t = 0.01$.

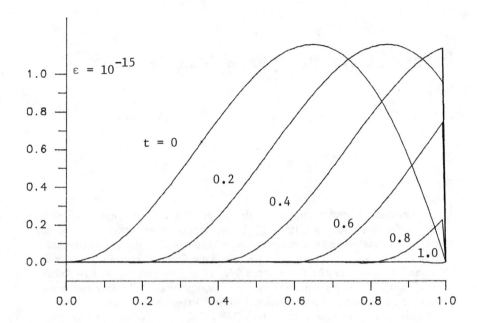

Figure 11. Approximate solution by the modified Crank-
Nicholson scheme with $\Delta x = \Delta t = 0.01$ and
initial data $u_0(x) = 2x \sin \pi x$.

We comment that the moderate mesh size used in the last experiment
makes our modified scheme rather promising for further study of singular perturbation problems on microcomputers.

REFERENCES
[1] L. BOBISUD, Second-order linear parabolic equations with a small
parameter, Arch. Rat. Mech. Anal. 27 (1968), pp. 385–397.

[2] E. B. BECKER, G. F. CAREY and J. T. ODEN, Finite Elements, an
Introduction, Vol. I, Prentice-Hall, Inc., New Jersey, 1981.

Using a Large Library on a Small Machine

DAVID M. GAY*

Abstract. Microcomputers are able to perform a wide range of scientifically useful computations. It is of obvious programming convenience to use "main-frame" software on a microcomputer. Most of the popular microcomputers have compilers available that implement some flavor of Fortran (Fortran 66, Fortran 77 Subset, or the full Fortran 77), so making suitably written "mainframe" software run on a microcomputer is straightforward (barring memory or addressing constraints). As evidence, I present experience in using the PORT 3 subroutine library on machines of the IBM® PC class. I discuss some tools that make using this library (of over 1500 modules and roughly 4 megabytes of source code) easy, even on a machine having only floppy disk drives. These include a simple archiving program and a program that tells what library routines are needed for a particular application. I also describe changes we made to the PORT 3 source code to accommodate Fortran 77 Subset compilers like those from Microsoft®.

1. Introduction

Personal computers now abound. Among the many uses they see are sundry scientific computing and data processing tasks. Fortunately, when obvious limitations of memory size and addressability do not intrude, it is often straightforward to make familiar main-frame software run on a microcomputer. Experience with the PORT 3 Library suggests that this is particularly true of programs that have been coded in Fortran with an eye toward portability. (It is likely true of other languages. C programs ([KerR78], [Geh85]), for example, often port easily. But my experience is primarily with Fortran.)

Some flavor of Fortran is available to most if not all of the common classes of microcomputers; in particular, several are available to computers of the IBM® PC class. Unfortunately, these Fortran compilers vary in the language they accept: some recognize only Fortran 66 [ANS66], some the Fortran 77 subset [ANS78], some the full Fortran 77 [ANS78]. Experience with PORT suggests that one can write Fortran code so it can be used with any such compiler (aside from the idiosyncrasies of OPEN statements).

*AT&T Bell Laboratories, 600 Mountain Avenue, Murray Hill, NJ 07974.
IBM is a registered trademark of International Business Machines Corp.
Microsoft is a registered trademark of Microsoft Corp.

Much has been written about portability of Fortran 66; [Smi77] is a particularly good reference. The next section discusses our efforts to achieve portability over both Fortran 66 and Fortran 77 compilers.

2. Massaging the Source Code

Following the tradition of the PORT Library's first two editions [FoxHS78], PORT 3 is written in the PFORT subset of Fortran 66 [Ryd74]. (This is not as grim as it may sound, for we have various preprocessors that handle much of the dirty work.) We do this because there are machines around — e.g. the Honeywell at the Murray Hill Computer Center — that still lack a Fortran 77 compiler. Unfortunately, some machines have compilers that do not recognize the Fortran 66 use of Hollerith data for character strings, and some of these, notably the Microsoft® Fortran compiler (versions 3.13 and 3.2), do not recognize the full Fortran 77 language. This presents a problem, because PORT library routines provide error messages by calling a routine called SETERR, whose arguments include a character string describing the error. Moreover, some of the output utilities need to compute output formats dynamically. Our solution was to instrument the source code with Fortran 77 Subset versions of certain statements as comments; these and the Fortran 66 lines they replace are surrounded by special comment lines that allow a simple preprocessor to activate the Fortran 77 lines and deactivate the corresponding Fortran 66 lines (or vice versa). For example, the PORT 2 fragment

```
            IF (I .LT. 1  .OR.  I .GT. 5)
           1    CALL SETERR(24HD1MACH - I OUT OF BOUNDS,24,1,2)
```

becomes

```
      C/6S
            IF (I .LT. 1  .OR.  I .GT. 5)
           1    CALL SETERR(24HD1MACH - I OUT OF BOUNDS,24,1,2)
      C/7S
      C     IF (I .LT. 1  .OR.  I .GT. 5)
      C    1    CALL SETERR('D1MACH - I OUT OF BOUNDS',24,1,2)
      C/
```

in PORT 3.

Changing Hollerith strings to character strings is straightforward (and automatic — with the aid of a suitable program). This leaves some problems with character strings in the Fortran 77 subset language. The subset language omits concatenation and the substring operator, and the only character-string expression it permits as a format specifier is a character-string variable. To provide dynamic formats, it therefore appears necessary to play games with EQUIVALENCE. For example, the utility module APRNTR prints lines of REAL data in format $1\text{PE}W.D$, where W and D are parameters. It computes strings used as the formats in its WRITE statements. The Fortran 66 version of such a string is an integer array, whereas the Fortran 77 (subset) version is a character-string variable *and* an array of length 1 character-string variables, EQUIVALENCEd together, as in

```
      CHARACTER*18 IFMT2C
      CHARACTER*1  IFMT2(18)
      EQUIVALENCE (IFMT2(1), IFMT2C)
```

IFMT2 is initialized in a DATA statement, but a few key elements are assigned new values when APRNTR is called. IFMT2C appears as the format in a WRITE statement:

```
WRITE(IOUT, IFMT2C) BLANK, ILAST, (LAST(K), K=1,NCOL)
```

In hopes of increasing efficiency with some compilers, the Fortran 77 versions of some PORT 3 optimization routines include PARAMETER statements for symbolic subscripts and SAVE statements for machine-dependent constants (obtained from a function call the first time they are needed). Since PARAMETER and SAVE are not in the Fortran 77 Subset language, these (commented) statements and those they replace are delimited differently than the lines that deal with CHARACTER data. The delimiting comments are as in [DenGW81]: "C/6" and "C/7" rather than "C/6S" and "C/7S".

The comment conventions described above increase the PORT 3 source by eight to ten percent and allow nearly automatic conversion to Fortran 77 or the Fortran 77 Subset. One detail remains to be done by hand: the "number of characters per word" returned by I1MACH, the function that returns machine-dependent integers, must be changed to 1 (by modifying the appropriate DATA statement). Of course, when moving PORT 3 to a different machine, one must tinker I1MACH anyway to activate DATA statements for the right machine constants. (One must similarly tinker the functions R1MACH and D1MACH that return REAL and DOUBLE PRECISION machine constants.)

3. Opinion on Source versus Object

There exists a considerable diversity of compilers, compiler options, and computing environments. Even single compilers often offer options that some people will find useful, others not. For example, whether integers by default occupy 2 or 4 bytes is a common compiler option, and whether floating-point arithmetic is done in software or hardware may also be a compiler option. So people can use the compiler of their choice, exercise options appropriate to their situation and, if necessary, adapt (say) certain input-output routines to their environment, I prefer to see libraries offered in source form.

The discussion that follows is relevant to organizing both source and object libraries. (If one receives only source, it will often be convenient to compile at least the frequently used modules and organize them into one or more object libraries.)

4. Organizing a Large Library

If there is enough disk space, it is probably most convenient to have entire libraries on line in object form. But many of the microcomputers currently in the field do not have sufficient space for entire libraries as large as PORT 3. Still, large libraries like this can often be used with such machines — it is just a question of how convenient this use can be made. (Once mass storage is sufficiently cheap, fast, and reliable, the following discussion will be irrelevant.)

How should one organize a large library for use on a microcomputer of limited disk capacity? Coming up with a single scheme convenient for all people may be impossible. Consider partitioning a library over several floppy disks. Well, machines vary in the capacities of their floppy disk drives, yet it is generally desirable to break a library into as few pieces as possible, as this will minimize diskette shuffling. Thus a partitioning that is convenient for a machine having higher capacity disk drives might be impossible for one having lower capacity drives, and a partitioning workable for the latter machine might be less convenient for the former. Rather than trying to decide on a single best compromise partitioning scheme, I think it better to devise tools that help partition things to custom-fit particular situations — and help one to use the partitions.

A tool I find helpful in this regard is *lo*, my "*Load Order*" program. It was mainly intended to automatically determine which libraries one must load with a particular program, but it can also help one partition a large library into diskette-sized (sub-)libraries. Given the names of some needed modules and the call graph of a collection of modules that includes the needed ones, it determines which modules of the collection are needed and sorts their names into an order acceptable to a one-pass loader. It does more than a simple topological sort: it keeps track of which libraries modules come from, and it attempts to keep modules from the same library together. It optionally reports which libraries are needed and optionally lists undefined modules; because it can run substantially faster than some linkage editors (e.g. Microsoft's *link*), one can sometimes save time by using *lo* to predict whether a linkage editor run will succeed. The appendix presents further discussion of *lo*.

An archiving program is another useful tool on machines of limited disk capacity. The idea (an old and common one) is to store source for many modules in one file. Because disk space is generally allocated in blocks, an archive may occupy substantially less space than the files it contains would if they were "loose" (i.e., not in the archive); an archive program may also save space by compressing the data it stores.

The archive program I use on our home computer is similar to the UNIX® *ar* program, except that it restores dates to the files it extracts, compresses strings of repeated characters, and maintains a sorted table of contents to permit fast extraction of specified files. (Having dates restored is extremely helpful.) A "man page" describing my MS-DOS® version of *ar* appears in the appendix.

5. Experience with MS-DOS

My experience with MS-DOS began in March of 1984 when my wife and I bought a Tandy® 2000. (A few months later we would likely have bought an AT&T 6300, but the 6300 had not yet been announced, and the Tandy machine has some advantages: quad-density floppy disk drives (720 kilobytes each), ability to address at least 768 kilobytes of memory, and a nice keyboard with the return key in the right place. On the other hand, it is still not possible to put an 8087 math coprocessor on the Tandy 2000.) We currently have a full 768K of RAM and are running MS-DOS version 2.11.

We bought several compilers, including the DeSmet C compiler [CWa] and the version of Microsoft Fortran (release 3.13) sold by Radio Shack®. Despite some deficiencies, I find the former convenient for making utilities like the above mentioned *ar* and *lo* programs. The DeSmet C compiler is archaic in that all structure components share a common name space (this is a real nuisance), structures cannot be passed as parameters, and there are no enumerated types. Other deficiencies are that its preprocessor does not correctly expand macros within quoted strings, case is ignored for external symbols, and the compiler only supports the small memory model (one 64K code segment, and one 64K data segment that includes all constants, variables, and the run-time stack). On the other hand, it is fast, produces good code, and comes with a symbolic debugger that is nicer in some ways than the debuggers available under UNIX. I kept encountering bugs and inconsistencies with UNIX in the DeSmet run-time library; by rewriting the I/O library, I managed to cut more than an order of magnitude off the run time of some simple programs — a big blocking factor helps.

Accompanying the DeSmet C compiler were a nice full-screen editor (called *see*) and a RAM-disk device driver (that lets one treat part of memory as a diskette). Compiling and linking go substantially faster when the programs and their intermediate files are on RAM-disk — it's a real boon. (Using the RAM-disk and DeSmet C compiler, I can compile, load, and execute the canonical "Hello, world!" program in 4 seconds — about 50% faster than I can using the Eighth Edition C compiler on an unloaded VAX® 750. Of course, for big enough source programs the VAX is substantially faster.)

The UNIX editor *ed* is a tool that I find very helpful on our home computer. Its regular expressions come in handy, and it can help offset deficiencies in the MS-DOS shell (i.e., the command interpreter *command.com*), such as its failure to expand filename patterns. For example, I recently had occasion to adapt a program of 20 or so modules written in a nonstandard dialect of Fortran 77 so that it would run on our home computer. I split the program into files containing one module each (in part because the Microsoft Fortran compiler produces large intermediate files, so that compiling a program module by module is sometimes the only way to go), with names of the form *.f (* being a string of alphanumeric characters). The shell script *make.bat* consisting of the three lines

```
dir *.f >foo.bat
ed foo.bat <edscr
foo
```

let me type just "make" to attempt compiling the remaining source files. The trick here is that *edscr* was a sequence of *ed* commands that converted the names of the files from the directory listing command *dir* into a sequence of commands (in file *foo.bat*) that successively compiled and deleted the *.f files until the compiler found errors in one of them (or all were compiled). *Edscr* contained the lines

```
1,4d
$d
1,$s/  *F.*/
1,$s/.*/for1 &.f;\
if errorlevel 1 goto done\
erase &.f\
pas2\
if errorlevel 1 goto done\
copy &.obj b:\
erase &.obj
w
```

The first two lines get rid of junk from the *dir* output, and the third strips away everything but the basename of each file (the part before the ".f"). The fourth through tenth lines substitute seven command lines for each file name; "&" stands for the basename of the file in this case. The "w" command writes out the resulting command file. See chapter 1 and Appendix 1 of [KerP84] for more on *ed*.

VAX is a trademark of Digital Equipment Corp.

Here's the recent history of the version of *ed* that I use. Andy Koenig modified the UNIX source, removing encryption, and made it run on his IBM PC. He then gave me a copy of the source, which I further modified a bit to make it read and write its subject file in larger blocks. Compiling it with the DeSmet compiler and loading it with my version of the basic I/O library, I obtained a version that is less than half the size of Andy's (mine is less than 14 kilobytes long) and that reads and writes its files more quickly. It could probably be made still faster by modifying it so its scratch file is written and read with a larger block size.

Another handy UNIX tool is *fsplit*, a program that splits a big Fortran source file into its constituent modules, putting e.g. subroutine `foobar` into file *foobar.f*. Porting *fsplit* was trivial.

Just as *ar* is handy for organizing source code, so is an object module librarian for organizing the object modules that compilers produce. (Under UNIX, the *ar* command is used primarily for this purpose.) I might simply have got by with Microsoft's *lib* program, but it did not come with any of the software (basic system, Assembler, Fortran compiler) I got from Radio Shack. A recent revision of the basic system did include Microsoft's *lib*, but I had long since followed a friend's recommendation and bought a librarian called Polylibrarian® (also *lib* for short) [POL]. It is rather more flexible and easy to use than Microsoft's *lib*. The important thing is to have some such tool.

It may come as no surprise that the first large Fortran program I tried running on our home computer was one that calls the nonlinear least-squares solver NL2SOL [DenGW81]. This successful exercise convinced me of several things: that using a large library on such a small machine might be practical, and that source and object librarian programs would be very helpful.

6. PORT 3 Under MS-DOS

PORT 3 is a large subroutine library, about twice as large as PORT 2 (its previous edition). Its source runs to over 143,000 lines and 4,300,000 bytes of Fortran code. (The latter figure excludes the trailing blanks and sequence numbers that appear on PORT 3 tapes.) Like its predecessors, PORT 3 is organized into chapters: a framework chapter providing service routines for handling errors, managing a run-time stack, and providing machine-dependent constants; a chapter of utilities and one of basic linear algebra routines; and application chapters that address approximation, ordinary and partial differential equations, fast Fourier transforms, linear algebra (both dense and sparse), optimization, quadrature, root finding, and special functions.

Because PORT is documented by chapter, it seems convenient to organize the source code by chapter, too (and it is so organized on the distribution tapes). When bringing PORT 3 up on our home computer, I thought it prudent to split the larger chapters further into pieces small enough that each would fit on a double-sided, double-density 5¼ inch diskette (capacity 360 kilobytes — a size then popular). I used *lo* to totally order the library, and somewhat arbitrarily picked points in the resulting order at which to split the larger chapters. (Phyllis Fox had tried to totally order PORT 3 by hand and had nearly succeeded; we had to shift only a couple of modules to bring it into the totally ordered form that distribution tapes now have — the form that a one-pass loader would require.)

Eventually I downloaded the entire PORT 3 library, and compiled everything but the

---

Polylibrarian is a trademark of POLYTRON Corp.

routines that use complex arithmetic: the Microsoft version 3.13 compiler does not recognize COMPLEX. (This exercise revealed a few problems with the source, which we then corrected.) Meanwhile, starting before we modified the PORT 3 source as described in §2, Leonilda Farrow began downloading it to her IBM PC/XT, massaging it as in §2 by hand, and compiling it with the Microsoft version 3.2 compiler (which does recognize COMPLEX). Unfortunately, the latter compiler has a bug requiring function parameters to be declared EXTERNAL before they are appear in a type statement, but aside from this, her compiler seems happy with PORT 3. Lately Brian Kincaid has also been running various PORT 3 routines on his AT&T 6300 (compiled from diskettes I gave him of *ar* files). His only troubles have been with the EXTERNAL bug and the tolerances in some of the PORT 3 quadrature examples — tolerances chosen for single-precision arithmetic on the Murray Hill Computer Center's old Honeywell and thus too demanding for binary single-precision IEEE standard arithmetic. In short, all the PORT 3 routines any of us have tested seem to run properly on our respective MS-DOS machines (modulo overly demanding tolerances in the examples).

REFERENCES

[ANS66]   *American National Standard X3.9-1966 (ISO 1539-1972), FORTRAN*, American National Standards Institute, Inc. (ANSI), New York, 1966.

[ANS78]   *American National Standard Programming Language FORTRAN, ANSI X3.9-1978*, American National Standards Institute, Inc. (ANSI), New York, 1978.

[CWa]   C Ware Corp., P.O. Box C, Sunnyvale, CA 94087; (408) 720−9696.

[DenGW81] J. E. Dennis, Jr., D. M. Gay and R. E. Welsch, *Algorithm 573 − NL2SOL, An Adaptive Nonlinear Least-Squares Algorithm*, ACM Trans. Math. Software **7** (1981), pp. 369−383.

[FoxHS78] P. A. Fox, A. D. Hall and N. L. Schryer, *The PORT Mathematical Subroutine Library*, ACM Trans. Math. Software **4** (1978), pp. 104−126.

[Geh85]   N. Gehani, *C: An Advanced Introduction*, Computer Science Press, 1985.

[KerP84]   B. W. Kernighan and R. Pike, *The UNIX Programming Environment*, Prentice-Hall, 1984.

[KerR78]   B. W. Kernighan and D. M. Ritchie, *The C Programming Language*, Prentice-Hall, 1978.

[Knu69]   D. E. Knuth, *Fundamental Algorithms/The Art of Computer Programming, Volume 1*, Addison Wesley, 1969.

[POL]   POLYTRON Corp., P.O. Box 787, Hillsboro, OR 97123; (503) 648−8595.

[Ryd74]   B. G. Ryder, "The PFORT Verifier", *Software Practice and Experience* **4** (1974), pp. 359−377.

[Smi77]   B. T. Smith, "FORTRAN Poisoning and Antidotes". In *Portability of Numerical Software/Lecture Notes in Computer Science 57*, Springer-Verlag, 1977.

Appendix: *lo* **Discussion and "man" Pages**

This appendix starts with further discussion of *lo* and ends with "man pages" describing *ar* and *lo*. The discussion starts with a sketch of the algorithm:

Lo reads its input files to obtain call graph information, does a depth-first search to break cycles (and discard unneeded modules), topologically sorts (i.e., totally orders) its input, and writes out the requested details about the sorted input. The topological sort is a variant of one described on pp. 258–260 of [Knu69]. *Lo* maintains a count of how many modules reference each module. Modules having a reference count of zero are eligible to be assigned their place in the total order. Because cycles have been broken, there must always be at least one module having a reference count of zero unless every module has already been assigned its place. Whenever a module is assigned its place, *lo* decrements the reference counts of the modules it references. If there are then any other modules in the same library having reference count zero, *lo* selects one of them to be ordered next; otherwise *lo* selects a module with reference count zero from the earliest possible library, where the input order of the libraries determines earliness.

Lo uses appropriate list structures to achieve an algorithm that should be a linear-time algorithm in practice (i.e., should run in time proportional to how much input *lo* has to read). The worst-case time is linear except for the above mentioned search for the earliest possible library, which means it is linear plus $O(\ell \times m)$, where ℓ is the number of libraries and m is the number of modules sorted.

The executable form of *lo* (*lo.exe*) is less than 17 kilobytes long. *Lo*'s compressed form of the call graph of the entire PORT 3 library is a little under 32 kilobytes long, and a list of the external symbols provided by Microsoft's Fortran library adds another 4.4 kilobytes. (This list is helpful in checking for missing subroutines — one does not want to hear about library routines whose use the compiler hides. On the other hand, having this list can help one avoid name conflicts with the Fortran library routines — Microsoft unfortunately has its Fortran library names in the Fortran name space.) With both *lo.exe* and the compressed summary of PORT 3 on floppy diskettes, it takes *lo* about 11 seconds (on our Tandy 2000) to report which sublibraries one must load (or which library routines one must compile) to use a specified PORT 3 routine. *Lo* reads object files or object-file libraries from a floppy diskette at around 5 kilobytes per second when extracting call-graph information from them (again on our Tandy 2000).

NAME

ar — archive maintainer

SYNOPSIS

`ar` key afile name ...

DESCRIPTION

Ar maintains groups of files combined into a single archive file.

Key is one character from the set `adrqtpx`, optionally concatenated with one or more of `vuc`. *Afile* is the archive file. The *names* are constituent files in the archive file. The meanings of the *key* characters are:

a   Add the named files to the archive file. This has the same effect as **r**, i.e., if the archive already contains a file of the same name as a file to be added, then that file is first deleted.

d   Delete the named files from the archive file.

r   Replace the named files in the archive file (or add them, if they do not already appear in the archive file). If the optional character u is used with **r**, then only those files with modified dates later than the archive files (if present) are replaced.

q   Quickly add the named files to the archive file. This is the same as **r** and is included for compatibility with the UNIX® version of *ar*.

t   Print a table of contents of the archive file. If no names are given, all files in the archive are tabled in alphabetical order. If names are given, only those files are tabled.

p   Print the named files in the archive.

x   Extract the named files. Each name may be preceded by a path to the directory to which the file is to be extracted. If no names are given, all files in the archive are extracted to the current directory. In neither case does x alter the archive file. If the optional character u is used with x, then only those files that either do not exist in the output directory or have modified dates earlier than the corresponding archive files are extracted.

v   Verbose. Under the verbose option, *ar* gives a file-by-file description of the making of a new archive file from the old archive and the constituent files. When used with t, it gives a long listing of all information about the files. When used with p, it precedes each file with a name.

c   Create. Normally *ar* will create *afile* when it needs to. The create option suppresses the normal message that is produced when *afile* is created.

NAME

lo — tell what routines from what libraries and in what order given routines need

SYNOPSIS

lo [option]... [file]...

DESCRIPTION

Lo (*Load-Or*der) reads *file*s describing subroutine libraries and object files. These *file*s may be a mixture of four kinds:

- object files (produced by a compiler);
- subroutine libraries;
- ASCII (human-readable) files describing libraries and object files; and
- compressed versions of the input *file*s from previous *lo* runs.

Lo determines the kinds of such input files by looking at their initial byte(s).

Additionally, if an input *file* has a name of the form @*flist*, then *flist* is taken to be the name of a file containing a list of files of the above kinds (or again of the form @*flist*). Under UNIX®, such a name is equivalent to `cat flist`. This feature is intended for the MS-DOS® version of *lo*, in which command argument lists can be at most 128 characters long.

ASCII files describing libraries and object files consist of a sequence of words (strings of nonblank, printable characters), separated by white space (blanks, tabs, newlines, etc.). Words of the form

*libname** specify the start of (object) library *libname*;

objname: specify the start of object file *objname*;

defname (not ending in *, :, =, or ?) specify that symbol *defname* is defined within the current object module;

refname? specify that the current object module references (but does not define) symbol *refname*;

objdef= specify the start of object file *objdef*, which defines symbol *objdef*. This is equivalent to "*objdef*: *objdef*" (except that *lo* stores the string "*objdef*" only once — this is relevant when handling large libraries on a small machine).

Input object files go into the null library (named "*"). Output from *lo* includes information about all objects needed by objects in the null library.

There is one special object file: the null object in the null library (object : in library *). References to symbols defined in this object are discarded immediately during input (and are excluded from the output if they were defined after they were referenced).

Lo recognizes the following options (which may be elided, except that if "n" appears in an option string, it must be at the end of that string). If no printing options are given (none of −d, −l, −o, −r, −s, −u, −v), then −ls0 is assumed. "Printing" is done on the standard output, with error messages on the standard error file.

−0   (0 = zero) Omit printing information about the special null object.

−c   Write compressed object and library information on the standard output, which should be directed to a file. Only the −0 and −g options affect the compressed output.

−d   Print symbols defined.

−e   "extract" input in ASCII form. This is similar to −c. It differs from −tlord in that input is sorted by library, rather than topologically sorted.

−g   group libraries into object files (to see the ordering requirements of libraries): treat libraries as object files defining and referring to all symbols defined or referred to by objects within the libraries (and discard object names).

−k   keep objects that define no symbols.

−l   (l = lower case L) Print the names of object libraries.

−m   Merge objects of the same name (and library). Ordinarily *lo* ignores duplicate objects.

−n *name*
       (or −n*name*) Make *name* needed: have the output include information about all objects directly or indirectly needed by *name* (where *name* does not start with @).

−n @*nfile*
       (or −n@*nfile*) Make all symbols in file *nfile* needed.

−o   Print the names of objects.

−p   Inhibit the default printing of cycles on the standard error. For example, if A calls B, B calls C, and C calls A, then by default you get a message on the standard error telling about this cycle in the call graph.

−r   Print symbols referenced but not defined in the objects included in the output (on a per object basis).

−s   Print library names that begin with "#", and print the names of objects included within such libraries. When there are both source and object libraries, this provides a way to have just object names defined in the source libraries printed.

−t   Totally order the input, and print information about all objects, not just those needed (directly or indirectly) by objects in the null library.

−u   Print the names of symbols that are never defined.

−v   Verify that the input files and libraries are in an order acceptable to a one-pass loader − print warnings (on the standard error) about objects (other than the special null object) that refer to symbols not yet defined.

−w   Suppress the default warning messages about redefined symbols and repeated objects. (Note that *lo* sees nothing wrong with different libraries having objects with the same name − as long as these objects define different symbols.)

EXAMPLES

Suppose p3 is a file describing the PORT 3 source, and you want to know which files from what parts of this source are needed to run DN2F.

        lo -n DN2F p3

will tell you this.

Suppose you have compiled some modules and put them into one or more libraries in the current directory, and you wish to make a summary file that *lo* can use on later runs to tell you what additional PORT 3 modules you need for some application.

```
lo -cw *.lib p3 >libinfo
```

will create summary file *libinfo*. The —w option eliminates warning messages about symbols defined both in *.lib and in p3. It is necessary to list your libraries first, so that the symbol definitions in them are recorded. If you want to make sure none of your libraries define the same symbol, issue the command

```
lo *.lib
```

Suppose you have an application involving all the object files (*.obj) in the current directory, and you wonder which libraries are needed and whether you must compile anything else.

```
lo *.obj libinfo
```

will tell you these things. If you want to know just about additional source files needed, use the command

```
lo -s *.obj libinfo
```

If you want to know just whether you need some modules not in your object libraries, use the command

```
lo -u *.obj libinfo
```

Some Fortran implementations, such as the one by Microsoft®, define a large number of symbols in their run-time libraries. It is often convenient to discard these symbols, especially if you want to use the —u option (as above), or if you are dealing with a large number of symbols. (The MS-DOS version of *lo* will handle somewhere around 2100 symbols; it can handle more if you discard the symbols in FORTRAN.LIB, as follows.) The command

```
lo -td FORTRAN.LIB >flib
```

will create a list of the symbols defined in FORTRAN.LIB. If flib is the first file that *lo* sees, it will include all these symbols as symbols defined in the special null object and will discard other occurrences of them. If, say, p3 does not already automatically discard these symbols for you, you can make a version, say p31, that does via

```
lo -c flib p3 >p31
```

Suppose you have a collection of objects, *.obj, that you want put into a library in an order that allows a one-pass loader to pick up all routines required from the library. You can have an acceptable order put into file zap via

```
lo -to *.obj >zap
```

This has the same effect as the UNIX command

```
lorder *.obj | tsort >zap
```

Suppose you want to know which subroutines are called by *.obj. You can find out via

```
lo -or *.obj
```

Similarly you can find out which external symbols are defined in bletch.obj via

```
lo -d bletch.obj
```

Except for output formatting, the commands

```
lo -rod *.obj
```

and

```
lo -tlord *.lib
```

are thus similar to the UNIX commands

```
nm -g *.obj
```

and

```
nm -g *.lib
```

Multiprocessor Microcomputers

W. MORVEN GENTLEMAN*

Abstract

Many microcomputer designs are bus based. Although the slots
provided were originally intended to facilitate addition of memory
and peripherals, they often allow processor cards to be added also.
Such additional processors can be used as alternates to the
original processor (e.g. the Sritek Microcard for the IBM PC), can
be used to provide special computational facilities (e.g. the
Marinco or DSP vector processors for the IBM PC), or can be used to
give inexpensive parallel computation. Special support software is
obviously required and, in the first two cases, is provided by the
manufacturer of the add-on processor card. For the third case,
commercial support software is not yet available. We describe an
operating system, which appears as a library of subroutines, that
lets standard languages be used in this third case. We report on
experience with systems based on Motorola 68000 family processors,
although our system is portable to other instruction sets.

Introduction

Microcomputers are often thought of primarily as computers that
are cheap enough for local ownership, perhaps even personal
ownership, thereby finessing the accountability and funding
problems often arising with central computing services. This
freedom can lead to more experimental uses and ultimately to higher
human productivity. Microcomputers are also often thought of as
computers for which superior man-machine interfaces are normal,
making computing much friendlier than with central computing
services. Through historical accident, microcomputers are far more

---

*National Research Council of Canada, Ottawa, Ontario, Canada K1A 0R8

This paper was supported by National Research Council grant #25968.

likely to support graphics, pointing devices, colour, multi-window
asynchronism, speech output, and so forth than are timesharing
systems. Microcomputers are also often thought of as being
physically portable, which can be a major attraction.

However, it is generally assumed that the advantages of
microcomputers are offset by severe limitations on the
computational power available for scientific computation. This
impression is partly due to the fact that many microcomputers have
used language interpreters, such as for BASIC, instead of the
compilers normally found on larger machines. It is partly due to
many microcomputers having too little memory. It is partly due to
the fact that the slow peripherals on microcomputers often affect
the speed of initiating a computation and the speed with which the
computation proceeds. It is partly due to the fact that many of
the microprocessors commonly used in microcomputers have no
floating point hardware and, because hardware coprocessors have not
been used, slow software floating point computation is necessary.
Each of these problems is gradually being eliminated. Sometimes,
on the other hand, the problem really is that the microprocessors
commonly used in microcomputers, from the 6502 to the Z80 to the
8088 to even the 80286 and the 68010, have less computational power
than the processors used in timesharing systems, indeed maybe less
even than that portion of a timesharing system a single user gets.
While more powerful microprocessors are coming, the problem
remains.

When the problem really is that a single processor is
insufficiently powerful, the classical answer is to try multiple
processors. That answer, however, has traditionally been regarded
as expensive and complicated, and not supported by available
products. This paper shows that this is no longer necessarily the
case.

Hardware

We start by observing that the hardware for multiple processors
for microcomputers is available and is not expensive. To go into
hardware in great detail would not be appropriate in this paper, so
the discussion will only be at a depth needed to understand the
background, not necessarily the depth needed to build a system.
Perhaps surprisingly, however, it is an adequate depth to be able
to configure a system and to use it.

Over the past few years a board level marketplace has developed
whereby, without requiring any electrical engineering knowledge, it
is possible to configure computers to take advantage of hardware
possibilities. I like to refer to this situation as "the hi-fi
enthusiast's approach to computing". The key idea is that
computers are produced with motherboards or backplanes that have
slots, which are standardized with published definitions. Third

party suppliers can then build and sell boards that are compatible
with these slots. These boards provide functionality not
originally available with the basic machine, perhaps enhanced
functionality due to technological advance, or perhaps enhanced
functionality for specialization that may not be of interest to all
customers of the basic machine. Peripherals and extra memory
packaged this way have been available for many years. What is
exciting in our context is that processors are now packaged this
way too, and for only a few hundred dollars. Originally they were
alternatives to the processor of the computer, then they were
coprocessors to be used as slaves of the main processor of the
system, and finally they are processors that can provide true MIMD
(multiple instruction, multiple data) parallelism. We note that
packaging considerations have dictated that these processors
typically come with substantial amounts of memory on the same
board.

Of course pluggable components of themselves do not ensure that
a system can be configured with little or no electrical engineering
- after all, integrated circuits and other basic components plug
into sockets. And so it is necessary to discuss the
characteristics of a bus, the hardware interface implemented by the
slot. Since the early 1970's, it has been common practice to
design computers so major system components, such as processors,
memories, and peripherals, were not connected pairwise, but rather
were all connected to a common system bus, that is, to a parallel
set of wires. Transfers between system components are then
time-multiplexed on this bus: a system component acting as "bus
master" claims a bus cycle, specifies the operation to be performed
(including addresses) and the system component "slave" to be
involved, actually transfers the data, then yields the bus to the
next bus master. System components must then be designed so all
interactions between them are in terms of such cycles, although
other operations can supplement data transfers - an important case
being interrupts. This style of design was popularized by the
PDP11.

Many designs for such buses have been produced, differing in
performance, functionality and cost of implementation. Some have
been proprietary and jealously protected, but many manufacturers
have found that having third party suppliers providing optional
system components for their buses is mutually beneficial, and hence
have published the specifications of the bus, or even undergone a
formal standardization process, usually through the IEEE. The
third party suppliers benefit by having a market for their
particular boards without having to build, sell, and support a
whole system. System designers planning new systems often choose
to use, or at least interface to, such standard buses because a
wide range of peripherals is then immediately available.

Early bus designs implemented the arbitration for which bus master got the next bus cycle by logic in the processor. Indeed, in some primitive systems, only the processor could be bus master, and all transfers were to or from the processor. However, higher performance could be obtained when peripherals could autonomously perform DMA (direct memory access) to transfer data while the processor continued computing, indeed when several peripherals could all be transferring simultaneously. This capability required allowing multiple bus masters. If timing synchronization was resolved, the small step to distributed bus arbitration facilitated not only multiple bus masters, but multiple processors. Most modern buses, such as Multibus, Multibus II, or VME, provide this.

An important exception to this trend was the original IBM PC and the IBM PC/XT. To reduce costs, the IBM PC implemented only an I/O bus, in that the DMA controller was combined with the processor, and only they could generate addresses: devices plugged into slots could not become bus master. Thus, although a board with another processor could be plugged into a slot, it would need to have its own memory onboard as it could not access the original PC memory. Because it also could not directly access other peripherals, it would have to work with the original processor to control them. Nevertheless, there were many practical examples of such boards, including: the Microlog "Baby Blue", which used a Zilog Z80 microprocessor to run CP/M; the Sritek "Microcard", which used a National Semiconductor 32016 to run Unix; and various "Turbo" cards that simply used faster memory and Intel 8086 or 80286 processors to run normal PC software. Although such "coprocessors" could be more powerful than the original Intel 8088, and several could be plugged into a single machine, reliance on the system processor to move data and ferry interrupts between them necessarily limits performance. (Some Turbo cards have plugged into the 8088 socket to get around the bus problem – which of course means they are no longer alternate processors.) It should be noted that the IBM PC/AT once again has a conventional bus.

Multiple processors are most interesting when they can cooperate to solve a single problem, and this entails communication and synchronization between them. Communicating between two processors is most easily and most efficiently done if they both can read and write the same memory. (The alternative, using some communications channel, is surprisingly similar to use, but typically has significant startup costs, bandwidth limitations, and protocol overheads even if reliable transmission is assured.) Early multiprocessors made all memory references across the bus to shared memory, but bus and memory bandwidth were an obvious bottleneck. More recent designs assume every processor has local onboard memory, which is used for the preponderance of that processor's memory references, not requiring any cycles of the system bus. Communication is accomplished by a processor making a reference across the system bus into the local memory of another processor, thus requiring the other processor's memory to be "dual port" (i.e. accessible both by the onboard processor and from the bus). Having all the local memory dual ported is simplest because then everything can be shared, but many processor boards dual port only part of the memory, because dual port memory is slower or because, if address space is limited, memory not accessible from offboard can be "shadowed" (implemented independently at the same addresses on another board). Another issue of dual port memory is address mapping: whether a given cell of memory is seen at the same address by all processors that can access it, or whether different processors see it at different addresses - the former simplifies using pointers, but the latter can mean all processors run identical software.

Synchronizing processors is done one of two ways, either through values written in cells of common memory, or through interrupts. Cells of common memory can be used as gates, or mailboxes, or semaphores, but always involve polling, which incurs wasteful overhead as well as delays of the length of the polling cycle. (Semaphores, and some versions of mailboxes, require read-alter-rewrite cycles on the bus.) Interrupts impose the overhead of a context switch, but do allow a processor to get another processor's attention immediately. Only a few processor boards are designed to generate interrupts to other boards, however, and standard buses are not well suited to have specific processors respond to particular interrupts; there are too few interrupt lines. The situation of the IBM PC is typical: coprocessors can only interrupt the main processor, not each other, though the main processor can interrupt any of the coprocessors, and hence interrupts from one coprocessor to another must be ferried through the main processor. Perhaps the ideal situation is where a processor board hardware monitors an address in the I/O space of the bus and generates an interrupt locally when that address is written to - this is called a "location monitor" in VME.

Though many processor boards for many buses are not suitable for multiprocessor systems, there are many which are. Suitable processor boards for VME or Multibus, with half a megabyte or more local memory, cost less than $2000. Coprocessors for popular consumer microcomputers cost even less.

System Structures

Having put together a multiprocessor microcomputer, how can we use it? The issue here is primarily software, although the options may be motivated by hardware characteristics, and of course hardware often supports only what was required for the envisioned software. There are basically three approaches: alternate processors, attached processors, and parallel processors.

The alternate processor is the simplest structure. Its primary value lies in the fact that a tremendous amount of software has been written for certain processors. The reasons for getting a specific personal computer vary, so many people have microcomputers based on processors other than these popular ones. Such a user of another microcomputer can tap the software base of the popular microcomputer if an extra processor in his microcomputer can emulate the popular microcomputer well enough that the software runs unchanged. This means the emulation is more than just using the same processor - screen handling must be the same; other I/O must be emulated at the same addresses; interrupts must be emulated, etc. Probably the first commercial success of this kind was the Microsoft Softcard for the Apple II, a board which provided a Z-80 microprocessor that ran CP/M software. Today the concept is well enough recognized that some manufacturers supply their machines this way from the start, e.g. the AT&T 6300, which is an MS-DOS machine, and the AT&T Unix PC, obviously a Unix machine, each have separate processor boards to run the other operating system.

There is, however, a secondary value to alternate processors. A microcomputer can be used as a program development workstation for cross development for a different microcomputer, one running a different processor from the main processor in the workstation. Most of program development, from text editing to source management to compiling, does not require the development system to be the same as the target system. On the other hand, debugging does require the target system, and if the target can be, or can be emulated by, another processor on the development system, a workstation with powerful tools in its native mode can provide a uniformly better environment for development than would the target system itself. Sometimes such cross development systems actually run the compiler and linker on the target processor too, perhaps just because constant folding arithmetic is done correctly, or perhaps because commercial compilers for the target system require execution on the target microprocessor. An example of an alternate processor for this purpose is the Oasys DS32 Co-Processor for IBM PC or other MS-DOS based system, which is a processor board with a National Semiconductor 32016 or 32032 processor and 1 Megabyte of its own onboard memory.

Implementation of an alternate processor system is straightforward. The coprocessor, by definition, runs as if it were the intended system. However, it is just a parasite, as the host processor actually has all the peripherals and ultimately is in control. Therefore, to yield the effect that the coprocessor is the intended system, the host processor must be loaded with software that performs the emulation. It would be possible to do the emulation at the level of operating system calls, with the system on the parasite modified so that operating system calls on it were translated to service requests executed by the host. More

often, however, the system on the parasite is unchanged, so the
emulation must be at a lower level, intercepting I/O requests and
emulating the expected peripherals. The host will also have to
emulate program loading or even system booting procedures.
However, there is only one thread of execution, as the host waits
for the parasite's command whereupon the parasite waits for the
operation to complete. (Asynchronous input, e.g. from a keyboard,
is the exception to this.) Host software is provided by the
coprocessor supplier, and successful systems appear to the user as
if the host did not exist at all, the parasite appearing as the
native processor.

The attached processor is also a simple structure, perhaps best
thought of as subroutines implemented in hardware. These
subroutines can be as simple as the floating point arithmetic
operators, as computationally intensive as signal processing
primitives, as substantial as solution of partial differential
equations, or as self-contained as computer graphics rendering by
ray tracing. The main processor performs the computation up to the
point where the special subroutine is to be called. The data
needed by the subroutine are then downloaded to the attached
processor, even the code to be executed may need to be downloaded
to the attached processor, and then the computation on the attached
processor is initiated and the main processor waits for it to
complete - after which the results are uploaded back to the main
processor, which can then continue with its computation.
(Optimizations sometimes tried to reduce the overheads, such as
performing a sequence of operations in the attached processor
before uploading the results, can make programming awkward.) The
overheads in performing such symbiotic computation are clearly
significant and only make sense if the computation to be offloaded
to the attached processor is substantial enough to mask these
overheads, and if the attached processor has a sufficiently tuned
architecture to perform its part of the computation significantly
faster than would the main processor. Signal processing boards,
for example those based on the Texas Instruments TMS320, and vector
processing boards (such as the Marinco or DSP), are appropriate
examples. The software for such specialized processors is often
tricky to write because of the architectural complexity, but
vendors of such boards usually provide not just libraries of code
for the attached processors, but also interface libraries for the
main processor that hide the existence of the attached processor.

The foregoing discussion assumed the purpose of the attached
processor was to do the computation faster, as is usually the case.
Attached processors are used differently by people interested more
in studying architectural features. Here the advantage is that the
interesting aspects of using a specialized architecture to perform
particular computations can be studied without one having to build
everything else, from operating system services to problem setup
and reporting - these can all be done in the main system. Many

experimental systems are available this way, the IBM PC serving as host to such diverse machines as the Ncube Hypercube or an array of Transputers.

However, both alternate processors and attached processors provide only part of the benefit of having multiple processors, because although limited overlap may be achieved, there still really is only one locus of control: only one processor is working at a time. The full power requires the use of the processors in parallel.

Although work in dataflow and in compiler optimization has tried to find and exploit parallelism in programs not explicitly parallel, the state of the art is that we are much better off if the potential parallelism in a program is expressed explicitly. One can argue that this is pedagogically preferable anyway. Such expression, most desirably, should not be too closely tied to particular hardware. Furthermore, it is not just the potential parallelism that must be expressed. Synchronization between asynchronous parts of the computation must be specified. Tuning is needed to balance the load across available processors. Expressing the startup of a parallel program can be complicated. One still has to do normal programming such as input and output, debugging, etc. Also the user of parallel processors does not want to have to learn (nor does the implementer want to have to build) too much that is new.

An approach that meets these objectives is to program the parallel processors with a multitasking system. This is the classical computer science solution, and there have been many proposals of how to do it - and apparently small semantic differences amongst them do matter. One style of proceeding is to invent a special programming language for this or to use an existing language with appropriate features, such as Ada. A different style of proceeding is to use a standard language and have the multitasking supported by the operating system. This latter style can exploit conventional compilers (providing they generate reentrant code, as most modern compilers do) and even can exploit existing subroutine libraries (providing they are reentrant, which unfortunately many are not).

A major difference with the use of parallel processors instead of alternate or attached processors is that the hardware is not usually sold by a vendor who also supplies the necessary software. Today, using parallel processors is likely to involve do-it-yourself software.

A Parallel Program Model

At the National Research Council of Canada, we have implemented a software system that can be used for such parallel processors.

This system is called the Harmony Operating System. It has been in daily use since 1983 in our laboratory and elsewhere. The software is portable in that with reasonable work it can be made to run on various microcomputers of appropriate architecture – most realizations have been on Motorola 68000 microprocessors although realizations are not restricted to that, and all realizations so far required the processors to share a single flat address space, although this restriction is inessential.

Because our concern is in running parallel programs, and we want to minimize the effort to achieve that, as well as to avoid senseless competition as to which development environment is better, the Harmony Operating System is used only for executing programs – program development is done conventionally in some other system. After programs are written, compiled, and linked, they are then downloaded to the parallel processors for execution. This mode of operation is quite common for realtime programming. It is not the only choice for Harmony – some people have used Harmony as an alternate processor with a Unix host, so downloading is fast and I/O is done through Unix, and another possibility would be to use the development operating system conventionally with one processor to build the executable image, then reboot all the processors with the Harmony program in order for it to run.

To take best advantage of what already exists, including the programmer's experience and subroutine libraries, Harmony appears to the user as a library of subroutines callable from a standard language, such as C or Fortran. These subroutines implement a multitasking abstraction. Although a central concern of Harmony is to support realtime computing, we will only describe here the aspects that relate to parallel computing.

A Harmony program is made up of many tasks. A task is like a subroutine except that once created, it runs independently of, and concurrently with, its father. Tasks can themselves create other tasks and can call subroutines – indeed the root function of a task, which is what the task starts executing, is just a subroutine in the chosen language. When a program starts executing, the system starts certain tasks, including the first user task.

Tasks are defined by templates. A template is a record defining which subroutine is to be the root function, how big a stack the task will have, and what priority the task will run at. The priority matters because in general there are many tasks on each processor, that is, each processor is multiprogrammed, and the tasks are scheduled in a natural break, preemptive priority fashion. A template is defined on a particular processor, and tasks created from that template run on that processor, but the template has a system-wide name so that the creation of a task from that template can be requested from any task on any processor. Since at any time there may be zero or more instances of tasks

created from a given template, task creation produces a unique id
by which that instance can thereafter be known. Since tasks do not
migrate to different processors, load balancing is achieved through
creating equivalent tasks on several processors and choosing which
one to give any particular piece of work. Tasks can not only be
dynamically created, they can be destroyed. Task destruction
implies the return to the system of all resources owned by the
task, and also the destruction of all descendents of the task.

   Tasks which are completely independent are rarely interesting –
normally tasks need to synchronize and communicate with each other.
In Harmony, this is accomplished by message passing. The
particular message passing semantics used are blocking semantics
which are equivalent to remote procedure calls. A task wishing to
send a message to another calls a primitive (library subroutine)
_Send, specifying a record in storage which is the message to be
sent, another record in storage into which the reply message will
be returned, and the id of the task sent to. Before the primitive
returns, the correspondent task will have received the request
message, processed it, and supplied the reply – during which time
the sender is blocked, i.e. prevented from executing. The
receiving task likewise calls a primitive, _Receive, specifying a
record in storage into which the request message is to be copied,
and the id of the task it is willing to receive from (with 0
implying receive from any). The receiving task is then blocked
until some request message comes. Another primitive, _Try_receive,
is similar to _Receive except that it facilitates polling because
instead of blocking as _Receive does, it returns failure if there
were no messages already waiting. When the _Receive or
_Try_receive is satisfied and the primitive returns, the receiving
task can execute to process the request, after which the receiving
task can call another primitive, _Reply, specifying a record in
storage which is to be copied back to the sender, and specifying
the id of the sender (as outstanding replies do not have to be
issued in any particular order). The reply is does not block, and
also releases the sending task to run again. Messages can be of
variable length, and indeed the sender and the receiver need not
agree on the length – the shorter length is actually copied.

   This style of message passing facilitates flow control between
producing and consuming tasks, and empirically is less prone to
many classical problems of multitasking systems, such as critical
races and deadlocks, than other methods of synchronizing and
communicating tasks. However, at first sight it appears subject to
another problem, over-serialization, in that, like subroutines,
only the sender or the receiver is running, not both. Thus it is
an important observation that the roles of the communicating tasks
can be reversed from the obvious, with the request for new work
actually being transmitted by a reply and the results being
returned by a send. In this way there is a paradigm consisting of
a task, that we call an administrator, which is sent work to do by

various other client tasks, but which is also sent requests for
work by various worker tasks. The administrator queues work,
whether requested directly by clients or generated as a consequence
of previous work performed by workers. It then replies units of
work to workers when they indicate their availability by sending it
the results of their last unit of work,. The workers can proceed
in parallel, only being blocked when there is nothing for them to
do, indeed the administrator also proceeds in parallel only
blocking when it has nothing to do.

The system is structured so that most common services, from
terminal I/O through a calendar clock to the file system, are
provided by server tasks, usually implemented as administrators.
These services, however, are not always part of the system, but are
only loaded if used - a minimal Harmony system is about 20 Kbytes
on a Motorola 68000. A server, once created, registers by symbolic
name with the directory task, which is another task created by the
system when the program starts. Then in general a task wanting a
service locates the server by calling the primitive _Open with a
directive specifying the symbolic name sought. This involves
sending a message to the directory, to match the server's name,
then to the server, to establish the desired connection. This
structure is not only configurable, in that only those servers used
in the program need be present, but it is open, in that the system
can readily be extended in a uniform manner by any services the
user deems necessary, such as perhaps a numerical adaptive
quadrature server.

The cost of a send-receive-reply cycle is typically of the order
of a millisecond, and the cost of creating and destroying tasks is
a few times this, so this model is suitable for exploiting
medium-to-large grain parallelism. Although the concept of tasks
is something new for the programmer to learn, and to be effective
the programmer must become familiar with the idioms described
above, experience indicates programmers do not find this hard, nor
do they find it hard to identify and express parallelism at this
granularity intrinsic to their programs. On the whole, such
programs look comfortably similar to the sequential ones they used
to write. Even debugging is no worse than normal.

Conclusion

The advantages of alternate or attached processors, their low
cost and the ease with which they can be configured and exploited
even by nonexpert users, means that personal computer owners
seriously consider such multiprocessor microcomputers when
appropriate. Our experience with parallel processors suggests
that, as software systems become available, this form of
multiprocessor microcomputer too is viable for ordinary personal
computer owners.

REFERENCES

Available products in this market change so rapidly that rather than cite those mentioned, it is more useful to point to sources such as the trade journals:
Computer Design
Electronics
Datamation
Mini-Micro Systems

which often carry product announcements and reviews,
as well as popular specialist magazines:

Byte
Computing
PCWorld
MacWorld

and many more which may be more readable and more accessible sources.

Various papers have been published about the design and use of Harmony, but the basic reference is the users´ manual:

W. M. Gentleman, "Using the Harmony Operating System", ERB-966, National Research Council of Canada, November 1984 (revised May 1985).

An Overview of Linear Arrays of Processors (LAPs)

MARTIN H. SCHULTZ*

Abstract

In this paper we present and analyze some of the issues involved with resource allocation in a Linear Array of Processors (LAP) computer architecture. In particular, we examine two test cases — the two-dimensional FFT and two-dimensional filters — to determine what we should do with our resources in order to get the optimal use of a LAP computer: increase the number of processors, increase the speed of the processors, or increase the speed of interprocessor communication. To address this issue, we examine the variation in compute time for the two test cases as we vary the number of processors while holding the other parameters constant.

1. Introduction

In this paper we present and analyze some of the issues involved with resource allocation in a Linear Array of Processors (LAP) computer architecture. In this discussion, we make the following assumptions:

- We have k processors, which are vector or pipelined.
- A fast bus with a bandwidth of B words per second and start up τ connects these processors to a large shared memory.
- In general, the aggregate speed of memory, m, is equal to the speed of the high-performance bus.
- Each processor's bandwidth to the bus is b, so that $\frac{B}{b}$ processors can simultaneously access the bus or the shared memory.
- Each processor can read (write) data directly from (to) either of its two nearest neighbors by direct interconnect at the rate of c words per second.

---

* Research Center for Scientific Computation, Yale University, 10 Hillhouse Avenue, PO Box 2158 Yale Station, New Haven, CT 06520. This work was supported in part by ONR contract #N00014-82-K-0184 and in part by a joint study with IBM/Kingston

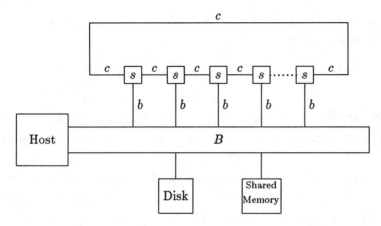

Figure 1: Linear Array of Processors (LAPs)

Figure 1 provides a schematic of this architecture.[1]

What exactly should we do with our resources in order to get the optimal use of our LAP computer? Should we increase the number of processors, k, should we increase the speed of the processors, s, should we increase the speed of the connection to the bus, b, or should we increase the speed of the interprocessor connection, c? In order to answer these questions, we want to examine the variation in compute time as we vary k, while holding the other parameters constant.

Let us call the run-time for a single processor T_1, and the run-time for k-processors T_k. Then the speed-up for k processors is $\frac{T_1}{T_k}$. As we let k approach n, the number of degrees of freedom in a problem, we would hope to find $\frac{T_1}{T_k} \to n$. Clearly, *linear speed-up* is the best we can do when relying principally on hardware for increased performance. This limitation is important to remember, because if we have a problem where T_n is some function $f(n)$ (e.g., $n \log n$ or n^3) the optimal speed-up would be $\frac{f(n)}{n}$.

In many cases, careful algorithm development can match or even out-perform the speed-up provided by parallel hardware. For example, suppose we want to do a Discrete Fourier Transform (DFT). Typically the classical DFT is an $O(n^2)$ algorithm on a single processor. By applying n processors, the best we can hope for from parallel hardware is to reduce the compute-time by a factor of n:

$$T_1^{DFT} \sim O(n^2) \Rightarrow T_n^{DFT} \sim O(n).$$

By switching the algorithm to a Fast Fourier Transform (FFT), however, we can reduce

---

[1] While the ensuing discussion pertains to all LAP computer models, we have made specific calculations for the Aptec I/O computer. In that computer, the high-speed array processor to bus connection could be the Data Interchange Processor private bus at 3 words/sec. For example, this bus could come into an I/O port of a Numerix 432 array processor. A low-speed bus connection could be a Unibus connection to a Numerix 432 host, which is taken as .25 words/sec. For the Aptec bus, the central high-speed bus is the Data Interchange bus with B equal to 6 words/sec.

this result *using a single processor*, to an $O(n \log n)$ run-time, which is roughly similar to the result for n processors running the DFT:

$$T_1^{FFT} \sim O(n \log n) \sim T_n^{DFT}.$$

As this example illustrates, a powerful algorithm can be as effective as powerful hardware. This is true for algorithms for every large-scale problem. It is especially true for algorithms for parallel computers for which we have the important issue of data movement as well as the other usual issues of arithmetic and logical complexity.

2. Test case 1 — The two-dimensional FFT

To display the importance of algorithms in parallel computations, we will present a detailed example of the two-dimensional $n \times n$ FFT, an algorithm commonly applied in image processing and spectral methods for solving partial differential equations. The two-dimensional FFT problem is difficult to process in parallel because I/O is crucial to its run-time. In general, the more work per data point there is for a processor, the easier it is to efficiently use resources — if each processor operates on the data for a long time, the I/O efficiency becomes less important. The two-dimensional FFT, however, requires relatively few operations per data point. If we are to produce a solution that uses our resources efficiently, we must balance I/O with computation.

To do this problem on a LAP, we divide the work into k pieces for the k processors when $1 \leq k \leq n$. Basically, we split the data by columns, with one or more columns for each processor. Thus, we have $\frac{n}{k}$ columns for each of the k processors. Once the data has been divided in this manner, we only need a three-step algorithm:

1. Do the one-dimensional FFTs in the y direction in each processor. We do these in parallel because each processor is doing its own FFTs. We can do these FFTs efficiently on any array processor.

2. Do a transpose of the data so each processor has $\frac{n}{k}$ of the rows. (This step is easier said than done — how we transpose the data is the crucial issue.)

3. Do the one-dimensional FFTs in the x direction in each processor, just as in the first step.

To calculate the efficiency of this algorithm on a LAP, we use the notation T_k^{CPU} to denote CPU time for a k processor system. Because we have the two FFT steps (FFTs on columns and FFTs on rows), we need a factor of two in the equation. In each of these FFT steps, we're doing $\frac{n}{k}$ complex FFTs. Each of these $\frac{n}{k}$ complex FFTs requires about $4n \log n$ arithmetic operations, and is normalized by s, the speed of one processor doing one FFT. Thus we get

$$T_k^{CPU} = 2\frac{n}{k}\left(\frac{4n\log n}{s}\right)$$
$$= 8\frac{n^2\log n}{sk}.$$

Notice that the time is normalized by sk, the speed of each processing node times the number of processing nodes. So, in terms of the arithmetic, we're getting the linear speed-up we would like: If $k = n$, we get an $O(n\log n)$ algorithm.

2.1. What is the cost of the transpose?

It is a simple matter to do a transpose of the data for a single processor; we would access the data by rows instead of by columns. It isn't so simple on a parallel machine because we have moved all the data when we partitioned it and sent it out to the processors. To do the transpose of the data, we will have to move all the data once again. We call this data movement I/O. In this case, the I/O is just moving data among the processors, not moving the data out to some peripheral disk. In order to truly evaluate the two-dimensional FFT on a LAP architecture, we need to know how long this transpose will take.

2.1.1. Moving the data via the high-performance bus

One obvious method of moving the data is with the high-performance bus. Each processor could broadcast its columns of data to all the other processors. In other words, we use a loop from 1 to k, where each processor J in turn broadcasts all its transformed data to all the other processors and each processor selects the necessary data points and stores the data for the FFTs in the x-direction.

This I/O operation yields the following result:

$$T_k^{I/O,b} = k\left(\tau + 2\frac{n^2}{bk}\right)$$
$$= k\tau + 2\frac{n^2}{b},$$

(2.1)

where complex numbers require two words to be transferred per data point, there are k processors, and b is the data transfer rate between a processor and the bus after a latency of τ.

In calculating the speed-up, we must always remember that there are two processes: computation and I/O. In this particular case, the computation declines by a factor of k. At the same time, however, I/O time increases — τ, the amount of time that we lose due to the latency to begin a data transfer, grows by a factor of k. These competing trends can obviously cause difficulty, as k increases, the total run-time (computation plus I/O) initially decreases, but then starts to increase. If we have a large system and want to minimize the run-time, it might be more efficient *not* to use all the hardware available.

2.1.2. Moving data via a shared memory

In the above example, we only use the high-performance bus, to a bandwidth of b, because we have only one processor broadcasting its data at a time. Sometimes we can use the bus to better advantage when b may be significantly less than B. One way is to use the shared global memory.

In order to insure that we use the full bandwidth of the bus, we define a parameter ρ such that $\rho \equiv min(\frac{m}{b}, k)$, i.e. ρ is the maximum number of processors that can simultaneously read or write into the shared memory. Now, to transpose the data, we take the first ρ processors and have them write their data into the shared memory. Then we take the second ρ processors and have them write their data into the shared memory, and so on for $\frac{k}{\rho}$ iterations. This loop uses the full bandwidth of the bus. Then we reverse the process, having the first ρ processors read the data that they need, except that they read it in row order instead of column order. Then the second ρ processors read the data that they need, and so on. Essentially this method of transpose is the same as the previous one except that we're using the shared memory to full effect instead of using broadcast over the bus.

When we analyze this algorithm, we get:

$$T_k^{I/O,m} = 2\frac{k}{\rho}(\tau + 2\frac{n^2}{bk})$$

$$= 2\frac{k}{\rho}\tau + 4\frac{n^2}{b\rho} \qquad (2.2)$$

$$= \begin{cases} 2\tau + 4\frac{n^2}{bk}, & \text{if } k \le \frac{m}{b} \\ \frac{2kb}{m}\tau + 4\frac{n^2}{m}, & \text{if } k > \frac{m}{b} \end{cases}.$$

Notice that m has replaced b in the superscript on the left-hand side of equation (2.2), because m represents the bandwidth of the shared memory, where b represented the bandwidth of individual processor connections. We have a factor of two in this equation because we have to read and write. This is an important distinction from the broadcast bus where we just broadcast. There are $\frac{k}{\rho}$ phases, and each of these phases is going to involve a start-up time of τ. Because ρ is the minimum of two quantities, we get two cases. When we have relatively few processors ($k \le \frac{m}{b}$), all the processors can read and write in parallel. Otherwise, they can't.

If $m \ge 2b$, moving the data via a shared memory is faster than using the high performance bus. For instance, when $b = .25$, $m = 6$, and $k \ge 6$, equation (2.2) gives us

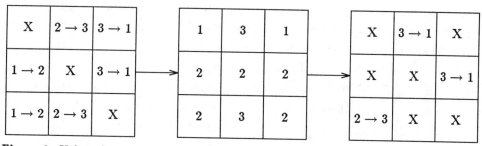

Figure 2: Using the ring structure to perform the transpose (a three-processor case)

$T_k^{I/O,m} = \frac{k}{12}\tau + \frac{2n^2}{3}$. In other words, this algorithm would be twelve times faster than the broadcast algorithm.[2]

Curiously enough, in order to speed up the performance of the total system, we may have to slow down the performance of one of the components. Suppose b is a free variable, and we can configure it any way we want. Notice that b is in the numerator in equation (2.2) and does not appear in the denominator. If we make b larger and speeded things up so that only one processor could read and write at a time, we would have to pay for k start-up latencies to read and k start-up latencies to write. We would actually increase run-time.

To decrease the run-time, we can slow b enough so that all the processors can read and write in parallel. So, we should decrease b, as long as $k \geq \frac{m}{b}$. Then, $b = \frac{m}{k}$ is the smallest b can be and still maintain the constraint. For that value of b, all the processors can read and write simultaneously, and we pay for only one start-up latency for a read and one for a write. The I/O time turns out to be:

$$T_k^{I/O,m} = 2\tau + 4\frac{n^2}{m}.$$

The dependence on the number of nodes disappears. This is the minimum run time we can have with the shared memory.

2.1.3. Local Connect

We can also transpose the matrix by using the ring structure formed by the neighbor-to-neighbor direct connections between processors. The two-dimensional FFT is a case where the ring structure, i.e. periodicity of the local connects, pays off. In this ring structure, we have an algorithm loop that goes from 1 to $k - 1$, and in the Jth step, we have all the processors send $k - J$ of their sub-blocks of size $\frac{n^2}{k^2}$ to their right neighbor.

For example, Figure 2 shows a three processor case. Processor 1 initially has the first column of blocks, processor 2 the second column, and processor 3 the last column.

---

[2] $b = .25\text{MW/sec}$ and $m = 6\text{MW/sec}$ are relevant to the hardware system components discussed in note 1.

Basically, we want processor 1 to get the first row of blocks, processor 2 to get the second row, and processor 3 to get the third row. Note that we don't have to move the diagonal blocks. There are two phases in this approach. In the first phase, processor 1 sends its off-diagonal blocks to its right-hand neighbor, processor 2. In parallel, processor 2 sends its off-diagonal blocks to processor 3, and processor 3 sends its off-diagonal blocks to processor 1. We can think of this basically as doing a rotation of the off-diagonal data. Now we do the second phase, one more rotation. But now for each processor one off-diagonal block is in the right place, so we don't have to move it. That means that when we do each subsequent rotation, we need to move one less block than we moved in the prior rotation. Proceeding this way, we wind up with the correct assignment of all the data.

Now we calculate the time required for the I/O. On the Jth step, the amount of the data we are moving per processor is $k - J$ blocks each of which has $\frac{n^2}{k^2}$ data. When we sum these, we get:

$$T_k^{I/O,c} = \sum_{J=1}^{k-1}(\tau + (k - J)\frac{2n^2}{ck^2}) = k\tau + \frac{n^2}{c}.$$

This expression has the same form as equation (2.1): it includes the n^2 term and the $k\tau$ term.

There is a common folk theorem that you can't do a transpose without a shared global memory or a bus. But we have just shown how to do it by using the nearest neighbor interconnect. This is a more complicated algorithm, and may be more difficult to implement, but it can be done. Furthermore, the I/O-time is similar to the I/O-time in the other two examples.

2.1.4. Bus Interleaving

We have seen three different ways of doing a matrix transpose: 1) using the bus, 2) using the shared memory, and 3) using the local interconnects. The running times for all three methods were more or less alike except that when using the bus, we couldn't take full advantage of the bus bandwidth. Now that we have shown how to do a transpose without a bus or shared memory, we would like to rethink doing a transpose with a bus without shared memory.

We now consider a method that we call bus interleaving, in which, in essence, we use the bus to evaluate a hypercube [1]. In this subsection we assume that k is of the form 2^t, where t is a positive integer, and $\rho \equiv \min(\frac{B}{b}, \frac{k}{2})$, i.e. ρ is the maximum number of pairs of processors that can simultaneously communicate on the bus. We partition the set of processors into two sets: the red processors and the black processors, each consisting of $\frac{k}{2}$ processors. Now we do a one-to-one assignment of red processors to

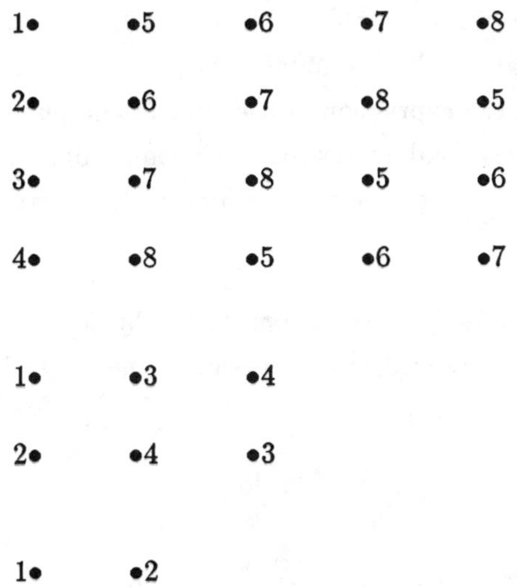

1• •5 •6 •7 •8

2• •6 •7 •8 •5

3• •7 •8 •5 •6

4• •8 •5 •6 •7

1• •3 •4

2• •4 •3

1• •2

Figure 3: Rotation scheme for 8 processors

black processors thinking of each subset as composing a ring. For each rotation of this one-to-one assignment, every matched pair (I, J) (processor I is red and processor J is black) interchange their subblocks $A(I, J)$ and $A(J, I)$ of the matrix A, ρ pairs at a time. Then we apply this procedure recursively to the subset of $\frac{k}{2}$ red processors and independently to the subset of $\frac{k}{2}$ black processors. Figure 3 displays an example of this rotation scheme for eight processors. When we have completed this recursive process, we have all the data in the correct processors, but in untransposed format. The final step is to take a transpose of every subblock in every processor.

The time required for the data movement for this scheme is

$$
\begin{aligned}
T_k^{I/O,BI} &= 2(\tau + 2\frac{n^2}{k^2 b})(\frac{k}{2})(\frac{k}{2} + \frac{k}{4} + \ldots + \frac{k}{k}) \\
&= \frac{k^2}{\rho}\tau + 2\frac{n^2}{b\rho} \\
&= \begin{cases} 2k\tau + 4\frac{n^2}{bk}, & \text{if } \frac{k}{2} \leq \frac{B}{b} \\ \frac{k^2 b}{B}\tau + 2\frac{n^2}{B}, & \text{if } \frac{k}{2} > \frac{B}{b} \end{cases}.
\end{aligned}
$$

The factor of two comes from the fact that matching processors at each stage must interchange their subblocks, e.g. first each red processor sends to its matching black processor and then each black processor sends to its matching red processor. The term $\tau + \frac{2n^2}{k^2 b}$ is the time required to transfer a subblock from one processor to another. The term $\frac{k}{\rho}$ is the number of times we have to do a block transfer, i.e. the number of pairs that must interchange data divided by the number of pairs that can interchange data in parallel. The last term in the expression is the sum of the number of rotations in each level of recursion. From the final expression in the equation, we can see that if we have enough processors (relative to the system parameters), we can take advantage of the full bus bandwidth.

We summarize the total costs of the algorithms using the above-mentioned methods of transposing the data, the high speed bus (T_k^b), shared memory (T_k^m), and the local interconnect (T_k^c):

$$T_k^b = k\tau + \frac{2n^2}{b} + \frac{8n^2 \log n}{sk},$$

$$T_k^m = 2\tau + \frac{4n^2}{m} + \frac{8n^2 \log n}{sk}, \text{and}$$

$$T_k^c = k\tau + \frac{n^2}{c} + \frac{8n^2 \log n}{sk}.$$

The above complexity bounds are particularly interesting because they illustrate the point that "fast talkers" that are "slow thinkers" may be more effective than "slow talkers" that are "fast thinkers," i.e. data communication speeds may be more important in the parallel multiprocessor environment than arithmetic speed.

3. Test case 2 — Two-dimensional filters

Our second example is two-dimensional filtering for image enhancement. We let M be an $n \times n$ matrix representing an image, i.e. each entry in the matrix represents a pixel. We apply a five point filter to M obtained by subtracting an average of the four nearest neighbors from each point:

$$(FM)_{i,j} = M_{i,j} - \frac{1}{4}(M_{i+1,j} + M_{i-1,j} + M_{i,j+1} + M_{i,j-1}).$$

This is equivalent to taking a matrix-vector product where the matrix A is the $n^2 \times n^2$ matrix representing the five point formula and the vector is now the image with the pixels ordered by rows. This particular matrix-vector product occurs in many other applications; in particular, it appears in explicit finite difference approximations to time-dependent partial differential equations. For example, if we were to discretize the heat equation in a square domain by means of an explicit time difference coupled with a central discretization of the spatial variables, each time step would involve such a matrix-vector product.

As before, we use a one-dimensional domain decomposition for developing a parallel algorithm for this linear algebra problem. In particular, we decompose the square

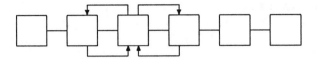

Figure 4: Data movement for a typical processor (inner loop)

domain into vertical (or horizontal) subdomains each of size $n \times \frac{n}{k}$ and assign one processor to apply the filter to those points in a single subdomain. Clearly, the CPU time to apply the filter to the entire image using a k processor system must be $T_k^{CPU} = \frac{10n^2}{ks}$. This means that as we increase the number of processors, we get optimal speedups in the arithmetic performance.

But when a processor is applying the filter on the boundary columns of its sub-domain it needs a column of data from the subdomain of its neighboring processors. This movement of the boundary data to the neighboring processors determines the time for moving the data among the processors. Our algorithm for doing the matrix-vector product basically has two phases:

1. In phase one, we move the data that is necessary so that each processor can apply the filter to *all* the data points that are in its subdomain. The data movement for a typical processor is shown in Figure 4. If we consider the Jth processor and let $u_l(J-1)$ denote the last column (the rightmost column) of data in the $(J-1)$th subdomain and $u_f(J+1)$ denote the first (leftmost column) of data in the $(J+1)$th subdomain, then after phase one, the Jth processor contains all the data from its own subdomain, $u(J)$, plus $u_l(J-1)$ and $u_f(J+1)$.

2. In phase two, each processor applies the filter to *all* the data points in its own domain. It has all the data points necessary to do this. Thus after phase two, the Jth processor contains $(Fu)(J)$, i.e. that part of the filtered image that belongs to its subdomain.

Let us now examine the time required for the *I/O* part of this algorithm. If we use the bus to carry out the data movement, we can have each processor sequentially broadcast its first and last columns to all the other processors. Of course, only the neighboring processors of each processor are interested in this data. The time to do this, $T_k^{I/O,b} = k(\tau + \frac{2n}{b})$, is just the number of processors, k, times the time for one processor to broadcast its data. This expression leads to

$$T_k^b = k\tau + 2\frac{kn}{b} + 10\frac{n^2}{ks}$$

for the total time for the problem. It is important to note that the number of processors occurs in the numerator of the I/O term and in the denominator of the arithmetic term. Thus, for small values of k the total time probably decreases because of the decrease in the time for the arithmetic. For large values of k, the total time probably increases because of the accumulated effect of the I/O. It should be clear that we could easily pick the parameters (design a system) for which we would get linear slowdown rather than linear speedup of the running time of the computation as we increase the number of processors.

We can now minimize the expression for the total running time by differentiating the given expression with respect to the number of processors and setting the result equal to zero. When we solve for the corresponding optimal number of processors, we find that $k_{opt} = O(n^{\frac{1}{2}})$ and that the optimal running time is $O(n^{\frac{3}{2}})$, i.e. $T_{k_{opt}}^b \sim n^{\frac{3}{2}}$.

Another way of handling the data movement part of this algorithm is to use the local connections. In this approach, we have two phases: in phase one, each processor sends its last column of data to its right hand neighbor in parallel; in phase two, each processor sends its first column of data to its left hand neighbor in parallel. The total time for data movement is now given by the expression

$$T_k^{I/O,LC} = 2\left(\tau + \frac{n}{c}\right).$$

This expression is independent of k, the number of processors. The total running time using local connections for data I/O is

$$T_k^{LC} = 2\tau + \frac{2n}{c} + \frac{10n^2}{ks}.$$

Clearly the optimal number of processors is the maximum for which this algorithm is well-defined, namely $k_{opt} = O(n)$ and this yields an optimal running time of $O(n)$.

Our analysis shows that by using local interconnections for data I/O we are in a situation in which the running time is monotonicly decreasing as the number of processors increases. Conversely, if we use a bus for data I/O, we are in a situation in which the running time may initially decrease as we increase the number of processors, but will eventually level off and then start to increase. Clearly, this is a situation to be avoided.

4. Summary

Finally, let us quickly summarize the main points of our discussion.

- With parallel multiprocessor algorithms, it is critical that the data on which we compute be in the right place at the right time. Therefore, in order to take advantage of all the CPU power we can bring to bear, it is critical that the I/O between processors be very fast. In fact, we have seen from our algorithm analyses that the I/O rates are at least as (and probably more) important than the arithmetic speed of the processors. This leads us to conclude that it is generally better to have a lot of "fast talking, slow thinkers" than a lot of "fast thinking, slow talkers."

- Domain decomposition is a general algorithm concept for parallel computing that is very effective if the number of processors is far fewer than the number of mesh points in some variable. If this is the case, we can be relatively sloppy about the I/O rates because there is an order of magnitude more computation than data I/O.

- Increasing the number of processors may lead to a disastrous situation. While it is tempting to think that we can can always speed computation by adding more resources, this is not always the case. In fact, it may be that the running time with more than one processor may be longer than the running time with one processor.

- Finally, algorithmics are an absolutely essential part of parallel computing. We put it this way: The algorithm is mightier than the chip.

Acknowledgements

Dennis Philbin edited the paper.

References

[1] Y. Saad and M. H. Schultz, *Data Communication in Hypercubes,* Technical Report YALEU/DCS/RR-428, Computer Science Dept., Yale University, 1985.

Optimization on Microcomputers: The Nelder-Mead Simplex Algorithm

JOHN E. DENNIS, JR.* AND DANIEL J. WOODS†

Abstract. In this paper we describe the Nelder-Mead simplex method for obtaining the minimizer of a function. The Nelder-Mead algorithm has several properties that make it a natural choice for implementation and utilization on microcomputers. Stopping criteria for the method are presented as well as a brief discussion of the convergence properties of the method. An algorithmic statement of the method is included as an appendix.

1. Introduction. We consider the problem

$$\underset{x \in \mathbb{R}^n}{\text{minimize}} \; f(x) \tag{1.1}$$

where $f : \mathbb{R}^n \to \mathbb{R}^1$ and the problem is to be solved on a microcomputer. The fact that a microcomputer is being used and the problem (1.1) is solvable on this microcomputer leads us to make several assumptions about the problem and the solution environment. First, we assume the amount of storage is small and, therefore, the number of variables, i.e. n, is also small. Additionally, we assume that computing derivatives of the function is not feasible.

There are a class of methods, called direct search methods, see Swann [6] or Brent [1], that attempt to solve problem (1.1) using only function value information. One particular direct search method that is used quite

*Mathematical Sciences Department, Rice University, Houston, Texas 77251. Research sponsored by NSF MCS81-16779, DOE DE-AS05-82ER13016, ARO DAAG-29-83-K-0035, and AFOSR 85-0243.

†Mathematical Sciences Department, Rice University, Houston, Texas 77251. Research sponsored by AFOSR 85-0243.

frequently is the Nelder-Mead simplex method presented by Nelder and Mead [3]. Additional references and several modifications of the algorithm are discussed in Parkinson and Hutchinson [5] and Olsson and Nelson [4]. The original method of Nelder and Mead is best-suited for our purposes.

The properties of the Nelder-Mead algorithm that make it appropriate for our problem and environment are its robustness, its simplicity in programming and its low overhead in storage and computation. We say the algorithm is robust because it is very tolerant of noise in the function values. Therefore, the function need not be computed exactly and it may be possible to obtain an approximate function value using many fewer floating point computations.

As we shall see in the following section, the algorithm is very simple to program. Trial points are obtained using very simple algebraic manipulations and these points are accepted or rejected based only on their function values. Also, when the number of variables is small, this algorithm is often competitive with much more complex algorithms that require a great deal of overhead in storage and algebraic manipulations. The low overhead and basic simplicity of this algorithm make it a natural choice for use on microcomputers. An algorithmic specification of the method is given in the Appendix.

2. Algorithm.   At each iteration of the Nelder-Mead simplex algorithm, $n+1$ points, denoted by $x_1, x_2, \cdots, x_{n+1}$, are used to compute trial steps. We will often refer to certain of these points based on the order induced by their function values, that is, at the kth iteration we have $\mathbf{x}_1, \mathbf{x}_2, \cdots, \mathbf{x}_{n+1}$, with $f(\mathbf{x}_1) \leq f(\mathbf{x}_2) \leq \cdots \leq f(\mathbf{x}_{n+1})$. A trial step is accepted or rejected based on the function value of the trial point and the three function values $f(\mathbf{x}_1)$, $f(\mathbf{x}_n)$, and $f(\mathbf{x}_{n+1})$.

The $n+1$ points used at an iteration may be thought of as the vertices of an n-dimensional simplex. In $\mathbb{R}^2$, for example, three points determine a triangle. We denote a simplex S_k, with vertices $x_1, x_2, \cdots, x_{n+1}$, by $S_k = \langle x_1, x_2, \cdots, x_{n+1} \rangle$. It is often the case that a specific vertex of a specific simplex is referenced. Thus, the notation $\mathbf{x}_i^k$ is used to indicate the vertex of simplex S_k that has the ith lowest function value. In Figure 2.1 below, if $f(x_1) = 10.0$, $f(x_2) = 7.0$, and $f(x_3) = 3.0$, then we would have $\mathbf{x}_1 \leftarrow x_3$, $\mathbf{x}_2 \leftarrow x_2$, and $\mathbf{x}_3 \leftarrow x_1$.

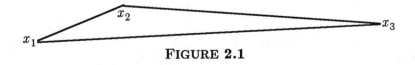

FIGURE 2.1

Trial steps are generated by the operations of reflection, expansion, contraction, and shrinkage. A reflected vertex is computed by reflecting the worst vertex, $\mathbf{x}_{n+1}$, through the centroid of the remaining vertices. Nelder and Mead compute the reflected vertex as

$$x_r = (1+\alpha)\bar{x} - \alpha\mathbf{x}_{n+1}, \tag{2.1}$$

where $\alpha=1$, and $\bar{x}$ is the centroid defined by

$$\bar{x} = \frac{1}{n}\sum_{i=1}^{n}\mathbf{x}_i.$$

The reflected vertex is accepted if $f(\mathbf{x}_1) \leq f(x_r) < f(\mathbf{x}_n)$, and the next iteration begins with the simplex defined by $\langle \mathbf{x}_1, \mathbf{x}_2, \cdots, \mathbf{x}_n, x_r \rangle$. Note that x_r has not been ordered with respect to the other vertices.

If the reflected vertex has a lower function value than $\mathbf{x}_1$, i.e., $f(x_r) < f(\mathbf{x}_1)$, then the trial step has produced a good point and the step is expanded. The expansion vertex is computed as

$$x_e = \gamma x_r + (1-\gamma)\bar{x}, \tag{2.2}$$

where $\gamma=2$. The expansion vertex is accepted if $f(x_e) < f(\mathbf{x}_1)$, otherwise the reflected vertex is accepted. Thus, if $f(x_r) < f(\mathbf{x}_n)$, then either the reflected or expanded vertex is accepted and the next iteration begins.

If the reflected vertex is not a better point than $\mathbf{x}_n$, i.e., $f(\mathbf{x}_n) \leq f(x_r)$, then a contraction step is computed. If the worst vertex is at least as good as the reflected vertex, i.e., $f(\mathbf{x}_{n+1}) \leq f(x_r)$, then the internal contraction vertex is computed as

$$x_c = \beta\mathbf{x}_{n+1} + (1-\beta)\bar{x}, \tag{2.3}$$

otherwise, the external contraction vertex is computed as

$$\hat{x}_c = \beta x_r + (1-\beta)\bar{x}, \tag{2.4}$$

where $\beta=\frac{1}{2}$. The contraction vertex is accepted if it has a lower function value than $\mathbf{x}_n$.

If both the reflection vertex and the contraction vertex are rejected, then the simplex is shrunk. The shrinkage operation is performed by replacing each vertex $\mathbf{x}_i$, except $\mathbf{x}_1$, by the point halfway between $\mathbf{x}_i$ and $\mathbf{x}_1$. This may be written as

$$x_i \leftarrow \frac{(\mathbf{x}_i + \mathbf{x}_1)}{2}. \tag{2.5}$$

Finally, the values $f(x_i)$ are computed and sorted along with $f(\mathbf{x}_1)$. This order determines the simplex $\langle \mathbf{x}_1, \mathbf{x}_2, \cdots, \mathbf{x}_{n+1} \rangle$ with which the next iteration commences.

If one envisions the simplex sitting on the surface defined by the function, then the operations of the Nelder-Mead algorithm can be thought of as the simplex tumbling down the surface. When the simplex has reached a point where further tumbling is not possible, the simplex contracts, or shrinks towards its lowest point, and the tumbling continues. Figure 2.2 below, illustrates the various trial points for the 2-dimensional simplex $\langle \mathbf{x}_1, \mathbf{x}_2, \mathbf{x}_3 \rangle$.

There are several stopping criteria that have been proposed for this algorithm. Nelder and Mead suggest halting the algorithm when the standard error of the function values falls below some threshold value. That is, the algorithm is halted when the following condition holds:

$$\frac{1}{n} \sum_{i=1}^{n+1} (f(x_i) - \bar{f})^2 < \epsilon_1, \tag{2.6}$$

where $\bar{f}$ is the average of the function values and $\epsilon_1 > 0$ is some preset value. Parkinson and Hutchinson [5] propose a stopping criterion based on how far the simplex moves at an iteration. They suggest halting the algorithm when the following condition is met:

$$\frac{1}{n} \sum_{i=1}^{n} \|x_i^k - x_i^{k+1}\|^2 < \epsilon_2, \tag{2.7}$$

where $\|\cdot\|$ is the l_2 norm, $\epsilon_2 > 0$, and x_i^{k+1} is the ith unordered point in the $k+1^{\text{st}}$ simplex.

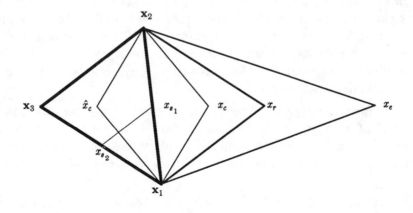

FIGURE 2.2

Stopping criteria (2.6) and (2.7) are very different. The algorithm is halted in (2.6) based on function value information, while (2.7) uses vertex information. Certain problems can arise with stopping criterion (2.6). For example, if the function values are very close, then the algorithm halts regardless of the size of the simplex. That is, the algorithm may halt when the simplex is very large. For an example of this and additional difficulties with stopping criterion (2.6), see Woods [7].

Objections to using (2.7) as the stopping criterion may also be raised. The main objection to (2.7) is that the left-hand side of (2.7) for a shrinkage step will be greater than the value for a contraction step, and we have observed that shrinkage occurs frequently when the simplex is in a neighborhood of a local minimizer. Woods [7] introduces the stopping criterion

$$\frac{1}{\Delta} \max_{2 \le i \le n+1} \|x_i - x_1\| \le \epsilon_3, \tag{2.8}$$

where $\Delta = \max(1, \|x_1\|)$ and $\epsilon_3 > 0$. This is a measure of the relative size of the simplex. Preliminary testing of (2.8) has indicated that it is a useful stopping criterion for the Nelder-Mead algorithm.

3.   Convergence Properties.   Although this algorithm is used extensively, the convergence theory is not well-developed. The only convergence results of which we are aware appear in Woods [7], for a slightly modified version of the algorithm, and in the forthcoming paper of Dennis and Woods [2], for the algorithm as stated here. The result of Dennis and Woods states that if the algorithm is applied to a strictly convex function and the level set of the function corresponding to the value at the worst vertex of the initial simplex is bounded, then the algorithm will converge to a connected set of points, all of which have the same function value. Additionally, each convergent subsequence of the sequence of simplices generated by the algorithm converges to a totally degenerate simplex, i.e., a single point.

Unfortunately, the convergence theory does not provide the desired result of convergence to the minimizer of the strictly convex function. In fact, Dennis and Woods show that this is not necessarily true under their assumptions. They show this by the following example:

EXAMPLE 3.1 : Let $c_1 = (0,32)^T$, $c_2 = (0,-32)^T$, and consider the strictly convex function $f(x) = \frac{1}{2} \max\{\|x-c_1\|^2, \|x-c_2\|^2\}$. The level sets of this function are displayed in Figure 3.1 as is the initial simplex, $S_0 = \langle x_1, x_2, x_3 \rangle = \langle (8, 0)^T, (-8, -4)^T, (-16, 10)^T \rangle$. It should be

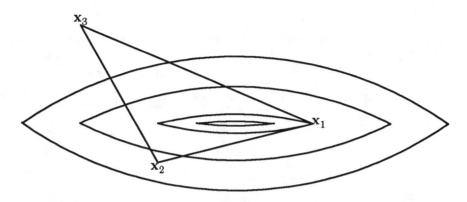

FIGURE 3.1

obvious from the figure that both the reflected and contracted vertices are rejected at this iteration and the simplex is shrunk. If the simplex were to shrink at every iteration, then the sequence of simplices would converge to the totally degenerate simplex $S^* = \langle x_1, x_1, x_1 \rangle$, which is not a local minimizer.

Dennis and Woods show that the algorithm can be made to converge to any point $(\alpha,0)^T$ depending upon the choice of the initial simplex. When $\alpha \neq 0$, the algorithm does not converge to the minimizer which is $(0,0)^T$.

4. Conclusions. The Nelder-Mead simplex algorithm is very well-suited for use on microcomputers. It is robust, easy to program and requires very little storage and information for execution. Although convergence properties for the algorithm are not well understood, the algorithm is used in many applications.

REFERENCES

[1] R. P. BRENT, *Algorithms for Minimization Without Derivatives*, Prentice-Hall, Englewood Cliffs, N.J., 1973.

[2] J. E. DENNIS JR., D. J. WOODS, *Convergence Properties of the Nelder-Mead Simplex Algorithm*, in preparation.

[3] J. A. NELDER, R. MEAD, *A simplex method for function minimization*, The Computer Journal (1965), Vol. 7, p 308.

[4] D. M. OLSSON, L. S. NELSON, *Nelder-Mead simplex procedure for function minimization*, Technometrics (1975), Vol. 17, p. 45.

[5] J. M. PARKINSON, D. HUTCHINSON, *An investigation into the efficiency of variants of the simplex method*, Numerical Methods for Non-linear Optimization, (F.A. Lootsma, ed.), p. 115, Academic Press,

London and New York, 1972.

[6]   W. H. SWANN, *Direct search methods*, Numerical Methods for Unconstrained Optimization, (W. Murray, ed.), p. 13, Academic Press, London and New York, 1972.

[7]   D. J. WOODS, *An Interactive Approach for Solving Multi-Objective Optimization Problems*, Available as Technical Report 85-5, Mathematical Sciences Department, Rice University, Houston, TX. 77251, 1985.

Appendix.   We now present an algorithmic statement of the Nelder-Mead simplex method. For simplicity, we have introduced the temporary variables x^k and x^t. In an implementation of the algorithm pointers to the corresponding vertices would be used. Various stopping criteria for the algorithm are discussed in Section 2 .

Algorithm A-1: Nelder-Mead Simplex Algorithm

Given S_0 with vertices $\langle \mathbf{x}_1, \mathbf{x}_2, \cdots, \mathbf{x}_{n+1} \rangle$, set $\alpha=1$, $\beta=\frac{1}{2}$, $\gamma=2$.

For $k = 1, 2, \cdots$

    set $x_i = \mathbf{x}_i$, $i=1, \cdots, n$

    compute $\bar{x} = \dfrac{1}{n} \sum_{i=1}^{n} \mathbf{x}_i$

    compute $x_r = (1+\alpha)\bar{x} - \alpha \mathbf{x}_{n+1}$

    $x^k = x_r$

    if $(f(x_r) < f(\mathbf{x}_n))$ then

        if $(f(x_r) < f(\mathbf{x}_1))$ then

            compute $x_e = \gamma x_r + (1-\gamma)\bar{x}$

                if $(f(x_e) < f(\mathbf{x}_1))$ then $x^k = x_e$

    else   set $x^t = \mathbf{x}_{n+1}$

        if $(f(x_r) < f(x^t))$ then $x^t = x_r$

        compute $x_c = \beta x^t + (1-\beta)\bar{x}$

        if $(f(x_c) < f(\mathbf{x}_n))$ then $x^k = x_c$

        else $x_j = \dfrac{\mathbf{x}_1 + \mathbf{x}_j}{2}$ for $j = 2, \cdots, n$

            $x^k = \dfrac{\mathbf{x}_1 + \mathbf{x}_{n+1}}{2}$

Check the stopping criterion.

Sort $f(x_1), f(x_2), \cdots, f(x_n), f(x^k)$ to

    obtain $S_k = \langle \mathbf{x}_1, \mathbf{x}_2, \cdots, \mathbf{x}_{n+1} \rangle$.

Interactive Graphics for Curve-Tailoring

JOHN E. DENNIS, JR.* AND DANIEL J. WOODS†

Abstract. We describe an interactive technique for solving multi-objective optimization problems. This technique is presented in the framework of the curve-fitting problem. A weighted norm is used as the objective function, where the weights are defined adaptively based on information obtained from the user. In this way, the curves are tailored to the user's fitting criterion.

1. Introduction.

This paper describes an experiment into the use of interactive computer graphics as an integral part of the formulation and solution of optimization problems which require multi-criterion objective functions. In this experiment, we are interested in curve-fitting on a SUN workstation on the Rice University $\mathbb{R}^n$ numerical network. We are working on a system to help a user with a parametric model and data of varying relevance to find an appropriate fitting criterion and the correspondingly optimal values of the parameters.

Our prototype has been developed for the user who has 1-dimensional data and a model involving 7 or fewer parameters. We are initially assuming that he would be content with parameters that minimize a weighted norm of the residuals at the data points. It is important that we do not require the user to specify the weights. We will explain in Section 2 how we deduce weights from the fitting information that we ask the user to provide. We obtain fitting information from the user by providing a graphical representation of the problem along with a pair of approximate solutions that

*Mathematical Sciences Department, Rice University, Houston, Texas 77251. Research sponsored by NSF MCS81-16779, DOE DE-AS05-82ER13016, ARO DAAG-29-83-K-0035, and AFOSR 85-0243.

† Mathematical Sciences Department, Rice University, Houston, Texas 77251. Research sponsored by AFOSR 85-0243.

are obtained by using different parameters applied to the user's model. The user is then asked to use the mouse to indicate his preference of pairs of models, we then rank the suitability of the corresponding pairs of parameter vectors.

1. The Problem.

We assume that we are given m pieces of data (t_i, y_i), $i = 1, \cdots, m$ and a model $y(x, t)$, where $x \in \mathbb{R}^n$ is the vector of n-parameters. We expect the user to furnish an initial estimate x_0 of the parameters, but it is not necessary that he do so. Our problem is to find a nonnegative weight vector $w^* = (w_1^*, \cdots, w_m^*)$ and a parameter vector x^* such that x^* solves

$$\underset{x \in \mathbb{R}^n}{\text{minimize }} \Phi(w^*, x) \tag{2.1}$$

where $\Phi(w^*, x)$ is one of

$$\Phi_1(w^*, x) \quad = \quad \sum_{i=1}^{m} w_i^* \, |y(x, t_i) - y_i|$$

$$\Phi_2(w^*, x) \quad = \quad \sum_{i=1}^{m} w_i^* \, [y(x, t_i) - y_i]^2$$

$$\Phi_\infty(w^*, x) \quad = \quad \underset{1 \le i \le m}{\max} \, \{ w_i^* \, |y(x, t_i) - y_i| \}$$

We refer to Φ as the criterion function and we allow the user to choose which criterion function is to be used. We have given an explicit criterion for choosing x, but it is in terms of w^*. The major requirement on w^* is that the corresponding values of $\Phi(w^*, x)$ be consistent with the order information indicated by the user for various values of x.

Specifically, if the user has indicated the qualitative information that for some p parameter pairs (x_{j_l}, x_{k_l}), $l = 1, \cdots, p$, he prefers the fit provided by x_{j_l} to the fit provided by x_{k_l}, then we say the weight vector w is $\Phi-consistent$ if

$$\Phi(w, x_{j_l}) \ge \Phi(w, x_{k_l}), \quad l = 1, \cdots, p \, . \tag{2.2a}$$

We also add the m *nonnegativity* constraints

$$w_i \ge 0, \; i = 1, \cdots, m \, , \tag{2.2b}$$

as well as the *normalizing* constraint

$$\sum_{i=1}^{m} w_i = m \, . \tag{2.2c}$$

By the structure of the available forms for Φ, it is clear that (2.2c) is consistent with (2.2a,b). It will be useful to let W denote the set of all $w \in \mathbb{R}^m$ that satisfy all of (2.2a,b,c). We will call any $w \in W$ *feasible*.

The constraints (2.2) ensure that any feasible w would be reasonable. We will resolve the remaining lack of specificity by asking that each w_i^* differ as little as possible from a previous selected value of w_i, e.g. $(w_{k-1}^*)_i$, where $w_{k-1}^* \in \mathbb{R}^m$ and $(w_{k-1}^*)_i$ is the ith component of w_{k-1}^*. For example, we might choose w^* by the l_∞ criterion,

$$\min_{w \in W} \max_{1 \le i \le m} |(w_{k-1}^*)_i - w_i| , \tag{2.3}$$

or the l_1 criterion

$$\min_{w \in W} \sum_{i=1}^{m} |(w_{k-1}^*)_i - w_i| , \tag{2.4}$$

or the l_2 criterion

$$\min_{w \in W} \sum_{i=1}^{m} ((w_{k-1}^*)_i - w_i)^2 . \tag{2.5}$$

The l_∞ and l_1 criteria each require solving a linear programming problem and the l_2 criterion requires solving a quadratic program.

We update the weights after every user selection. That is, the user compares a pair of parameters and this provides a single constraint of the form given in (2.2a). If our current weights satisfy this constraint, then the weights are unchanged. If the new constraint is not satisfied by the current set of weights, then the linear programming problems (2.3) and (2.4) and the quadratic programming problem (2.5) can be solved efficiently by using a dual method. For problems (2.3) and (2.4), the dual method of Lemke [6] is used, see Murty [8] or Ignizio [5]. The dual problem for problem (2.5) is also a quadratic programming problem and a solution technique for this problem is presented by Woods [10]. For a general discussion of duality see Luenberger [7].

2. The Solution.

It would be conceivable to generate some random parameter values, ask the user to rank the corresponding fits, solve for weights w^* using one of the criteria of the last section, and then apply some library optimizer to find an x^* that minimizes $\Phi(w^*, x)$. We favor another scheme which asks for user rankings that are used to improve the current parameter estimates. We believe that our scheme will be more efficient and will find better weights because it bases Φ-consistency on comparisons more interesting to the user.

We generate successive parameter values using the Nelder-Mead [9] simplex algorithm. This algorithm is known to be efficient for $n \leq 5$ and it is extremely tolerant of inaccuracy in the objective function values. We will not give details of the algorithm here (see [1], [2], [3], [4]), but it is useful to point out that the algorithm is iterative and that each iterate is not a point but is an n-simplex of parameters characterized by its $n+1$ vertices.

At each iteration, the only values of the objective function are at the vertices and they are used only to label the best, worst and next-worst vertices. In other words, the function values are not used except to provide ranking information. Since we do not know w^*, we can not evaluate $\Phi(w^*, x)$ at the vertices to obtain this information, so we get it directly by asking the user to rank the fits corresponding to the vertices of the simplex.

Of course, we could conceive of identifying the parameters independent of any assumed form for Φ by this scheme alone. It is possible to do so, however, the current version of the software has the capability to find the w^* if the user has been Φ-consistent. It is then possible to use a library optimizer with the Φ-consistent w^*. We have various techniques to deal with the possibility of the user's choices not being Φ-consistent.

To deal with inconsistencies in the user's ranking information we first identify the set of inconsistent constraints and ask the user to rerank the sets of parameters that were used to formulate these constraints. If we are still unable to produce a nonempty feasible set W, then we consider different criterion functions Φ from a predefined set. If there exists no feasible set W for each of the criterion functions, then we continue with the solution process via the Nelder-Mead simplex algorithm based on the user's preferences. We have considered other methods for dealing with inconsistent user information, but have not yet implemented them, see Woods [10] for details.

To generate an initial simplex we ask the user to provide an initial guess, x_0. We then display the curve that the model and x_0 provide and ask the user to indicate regions where the fit is inadequate. We then increase the weights for the data points in that region, starting from $w^* = (1, 1, \cdots, 1)^T$, and perform just enough iterations of the library optimizer to find a better point with these weights. The user is then asked which of the two models is better. This process is repeated, using the best available approximation as the initial guess to the library optimizer, until a nondegenerate initial simplex is defined.

3. Current Work. There are several reasons why we want to proceed to the stage of assuming a form like (2.1) and then to finding weights. We think it would be an interesting part of the data analysis for the user to have weights which he arrived at adaptively as a part of the analysis rather

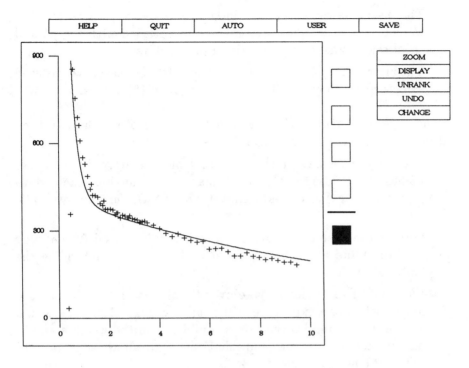

FIGURE 1

than by *a priori* assignment or by ranking plots that were chosen artificially. Once he has weights w^*, then similar data can be analyzed directly using our system in automatic mode to interface to a library optimization routine without redoing the interactive Nelder-Mead portion which we call *user* mode, or else user mode could be entered at an advanced stage. See Figure 1.

In fact, the user will be able to enter user mode with his *a priori* estimates of the weights. Our favorite reason to find weights adaptively is that we believe that comparisons at the Nelder-Mead vertex points are likely to point up inconsistencies in improperly assigned weights and lead to a redefining of the weights so that they are feasible. We expect one of three results if the Nelder-Mead process goes on long enough:

(1)   The user is satisfied with the fit found in *user* mode and the session ends with the 'optimal' parameters. It will also be possible for the user to obtain the weights that resulted from his selections if his rankings were consistent.

(2)   The user allows *automatic* mode to take over after feasible
           weights are found and, we presume, is satisfied with the fit and
           the session ends with the optimal parameters.

(3)   The user makes inconsistent choices. In this case, we proceed
           as described above until either result (1) or (2) occurs.

There are many other features of the experiment, some of which have been
implemented. These options include such items as:

(4)   Making the display of the data and plots exactly like the user
           wishes by adding axes, tick marks, by having each data
           represented by error bars that represent the current weights,
           etc.

(5)   Letting the user decide which norm should be used for defining
           Φ in (2.1) and also which form should be used to determine the
           'optimal' weights.

(6)   We would like to slowly take over for the user. We will put the
           mouse where we expect he will rank the next plot. This would
           enable us to build up the user's confidence in the weights and in
           our procedure to the end that he will allow a shift into
           automatic mode.

REFERENCES

[1]   M. AVRIEL, *Nonlinear Programming: Analysis and Methods*, Prentice-
       Hall, Englewood Cliffs, N.J., 1976.

[2]   M. S. CACECI, W.P. CACHERIS, *Fitting curves to data*, BYTE, May
       1984, pp.340-362.

[3]   J. E. DENNIS JR., D. J. WOODS, *Optimization on Microcomputers:
       The Nelder-Mead Simplex Algorithm*, these proceedings.

[4]   R. FLETCHER, *Practical Methods of Optimization, Vol 1,
       Unconstrained Optimization*, John Wiley and Sons, New York, 1980.

[5]   J. P. IGNIZIO, *Linear Programming in Single- & Multiple- Objective
       Systems*, Prentice-Hall, Englewood Cliffs, New Jersey, 1982.

[6]   C. E. LEMKE, *The dual method of solving the linear programming
       problem*, Naval Res. Logist. Quart. (1954), Vol. 1, p. 36.

[7]   D. G. LUENBERGER, *Introduction to Linear and Nonlinear
       Programming*, Addison-Wesley, Reading, Massachusetts, 1973.

[8]   K. G. MURTY, *Linear and Combinatorial Programming*, John Wiley &
       Sons, New York, 1976.

[9]   J. A. NELDER, R. MEAD, *A simplex method for function minimization*, The Computer Journal (1965), Vol. 7, p. 308.

[10] D. J. WOODS, *An Interactive Approach for Solving Multi-Objective Optimization Problems*, PhD. dissertation, Available as Technical Report 85-5, Mathematical Sciences Department, Rice University, Houston, TX. 77251, 1985.

Using Supercomputers as Attached Processors*

OLIVER A. MCBRYAN†

Abstract. We have developed software that allows one or more supercomputers to be used as an attached processor by programs running on a mini-computer. In typical use, programs are run as distributed tasks, with the supercomputer performing floating-point intensive computation and the mini-computer providing access to the richer set of software and languages typically available on such machines.

In one application, a 200,000 line C program running on a VAX 780 used a CRAY supercomputer to solve systems of linear equations at high speed, resulting in a 5-fold speedup in execution time on the VAX.

The same software is used to distribute a computation over several mini-computers or work-stations on a local area network. In this application one computer acts as the *master,* distributing computational tasks to the other *slave* processors in parallel.

A third application involves an FPS-164 array processor which is tightly coupled to a VAX/780. Using the software described, the FPS-164 is made available to other computers on a local area network, including machines running UNIX or other operating systems for which FPS-164 software is not available. A similar application provides access to an Alliant multiprocessor from a network of minicomputers and work-stations.

* Research supported in part by DOE contract DE-ACO2-76ER03077 and by NSF grant DMS-83-12229.
† C-3, MS-B265, Los Alamos National Laboratory Los Alamos, NM 87545.
  Permanent address: Courant Institute, 251 Mercer Street, New York, NY 10012.

1. Introduction

We have developed software that allows a supercomputer (e.g. a CRAY) to be used as an attached processor by a host computer running the UNIX operating system (e.g. a VAX, Pyramid or SUN work-station). Programs running on the host may make calls to the supercomputer to perform compute-intensive tasks such as solution of large systems of linear equations. See Figure 1 for an illustration. The software in fact allows several CRAY computers to be run either as a pipeline or in parallel, see Figure 2 and Figure 3, and provides appropriate synchronization primitives which are robust relative to a variety of possible system failures. We have also used the software to allow several VAX 11/780 computers to operate in parallel and more generally to allow a main program running on a mini-computer to access a variety of computing facilities such as other mini-computers, a remote FPS 164 array processor, or an Alliant FX/8 parallel vector processor. See Figure 4 for an example involving an array processor. This software has been run on a wide diversity of machines from at least 10 different manufacturers.

Given the relative computing power of a VAX and a CRAY computer, it might appear pointless to distribute a program between these two machines. Our initial motivation came from the desire to harness the computing power of the CRAY for some large fluid mechanics programs which could not run directly on the CRAY. These programs, consisting of approximately 200,000 lines of C, could not be compiled on the CRAY due to the lack of a suitable CRAY C compiler at that time. Furthermore, even with availability of a CRAY C compiler, the small memories of the CRAY-1 and CRAY-XMP machines would have greatly limited the simulations that could be performed with this program, whereas on mini-computers with virtual memories large simulations could be attempted.

Several possibilities were considered for getting the application to run on the CRAY. Because of the size of the programs, it was not practical to translate the codes into Fortran, much less to further modify the code to access a Solid State Disk (SSD). However, run-time profiling of the programs indicated that execution time was dominated by a relatively small segment of code, consisting of an algebraic equation solver. The algebraic solver was then rewritten in Fortran. In the distributed version of the program, the algebraic solver runs on the CRAY while the remainder of the program executes on the VAX.

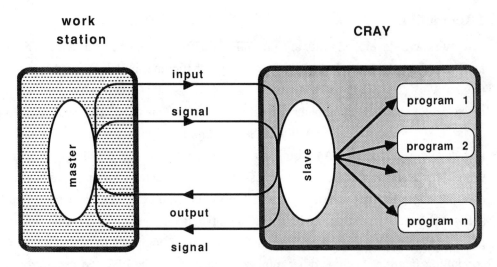

Figure 1: The Work Station acts as Master with the CRAY as an attached Slave processor.   An input data file is sent to the CRAY followed by a signal file.   After execution of the requested CRAY sub-program, output data is returned to the Work Station followed by another signal file.

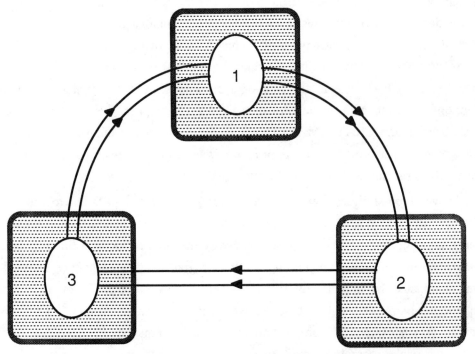

Figure 2: Processor 1 sends data and signal files to processor 2 which in turn sends its output to processor 3.   Finally processor 3 sends its data back to processor 1.   A ring of arbitrary size is easily implemented using the software described here.

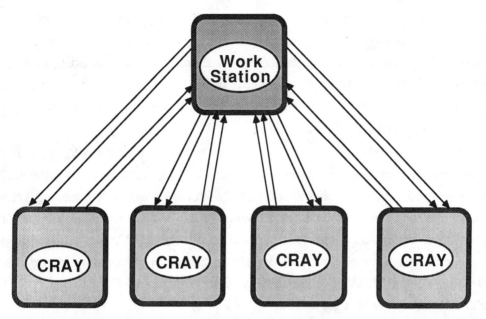

Figure 3: Here a single application on a work station uses 4 CRAY computers as attached processors, exchanging data and signal files with each.   The name space for signal files allows such multiple exchanges to take place safely.   Similarly several work-stations may utilize a single CRAY with safety.

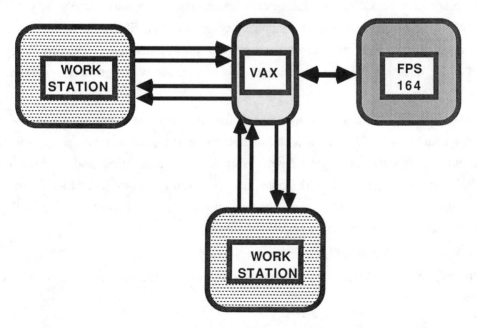

Figure 4: An FPS 164 Array Processor is tightly coupled to a VAX computer.   Using the network software, programs on various work-stations or other computers can access the FPS 164 by communicating with a process on the VAX.

Communication between the machines, including synchronization, parameter passing and data sharing, is accomplished over a high-speed network. To allow for a general and portable network interface, we have assumed only the existence of one network operating system primitive: a utility to send a named file to a specified location on another machine. Beyond this, all of the software involved is written in portable Fortran 77 or C.

We describe this software in detail in the following sections. We have previously given a brief report of some of this work in a Los Alamos Annual Report[1]. We have also developed related software that provides a UNIX operating system interface to the CRAY. This allows a mini-computer or work-station user to perform all editing, compilation and job submission for the CRAY on a user-friendly machine, which we have found to provide an enormous productivity increase over direct use of the CRAY in program development situations. For further details we refer to our paper on that subject[2].

2. Data Communication and Synchronization

Parameters and shared data are passed in files between machines. Due to the possibility of network failure during data transmission (the files are typically multi-megabyte sized), detection of the appearance of the data file is an unreliable synchronization primitive. Instead we typically send a second *signal* file after completion of the data transfer, and detection of this second file is our primary synchronization primitive.

As an added safeguard, the signal file contains the name and size of its corresponding data file, and in addition it contains the address of its originator, the address to which the results of the processing are to be transferred, and the name of a signal file to be returned with those results. Addresses are constructed from a machine name, a separator, a directory name and a filename. This allows specification of a file on most operating systems.

While the details of the communication facilities are complex, their use is extremely simple. A typical program on the work-station or VAX would take the form:

```
init_computation();
init_network(net);
while (more_to_do()) {
        start_local_computation();
        create_input(net);
        send_input(net);
        receive_output(net);
        finish_local_computation();
}
```

Here *init_computation* () performs normal initialization of the computational task, while *init_network* () initializes the communication specifics by specifying various data such as the name of the remote machine, and the method to be used to transfer files - all of this information is stored in the data structure *net*, see the following section. The loop performs the computational work, perhaps a time step in a fluid dynamics code. The computation is split into three parts with the middle part performed on the remote machine.

The three communication calls *create_input* (), *send_input* () and *receive_output* () handle all of the issues of reliable data transfer, such as waiting for rebooting of a remote machine that is down. These subroutines also handle the job of creating signal files, detection of signal files and of compiling timing statistics on the various phases of the communication. When results are returned to the calling program they are accompanied by a detailed breakdown of time spent creating, sending and reading data files on each machine as well as the time spent in processing on the remote machine. Both cpu and wall clock times are reported for each of these events. By initializing several different *net* data structures at the start, more than one remote machine may be harnessed simultaneously. Asynchronous usage is also possible - the local program may proceed with other work while the remote machine(s) perform their computations.

In the following subsections we describe these communications facilities in more detail. For convenience we describe the C language interface, although the routines can also be called from Fortran.

2.1. Top Level Communication Facilities

The communications routines are structured as a hierarchy several layers deep, of which the top-most layer consists of the three routines introduced above. The purpose of the hierarchy is to provide simplicity at the user level as well as portability among machine types and data transfer protocols. A common thread between these levels is provided by a network data structure which is passed between all levels.

Information describing a complete communication with a remote machine is stored in the *NETSPEC* data structure:

```
struct NETSPEC {
        char *src_mach;              /* Name of Source Machine */
        char *dest_mach;            /* Name of Destination Machine */
        char *src_dir;              /* Name of Directory on Source Machine */
        char *dest_dir;             /* Name of Directory on Destination Machine */
        char *iname;                /* File part of input filename */
        char *oname;                /* File part of output filename */
        char *isname;               /* File part of input signal filename */
        char *osname;               /* File part of output signal filename */
        char *finame;               /* Full name of input filename on src_mach */
        char *foname;               /* Full name of output filename on src_mach */
        char *fisname;              /* Full name of input signal filename */
        char *fosname;              /* Full name of output signal filename */
        char *command;              /* Command executed on dest_mach if non-empty */
        int (*input_func)();        /* Function called to write input file */
        int (*output_func)();       /* Function called to read output file */
        int (*send_func)();         /* Function to send files to dest_mach */
        int (*retrieve_func)();     /* Function to retrieve files from dest_mach */
        int save_input;             /* Saves input file if nonzero */
        int save_output;            /* Saves output file if nonzero */
        int debug;                  /* Turns on debugging if non-zero */
        struct Time_data loc;       /* Time statistics on local machine */
        struct Time_data reml;      /* Time statistics on remote machine */
    };
```

The NETSPEC data structure contains a description of a file interaction between two machines called the source and destination machines. In the following, *net* will denote a pointer to a NETSPEC structure and we refer to the source and destination machines as machine *a* and machine *b*. The primary data in the NETSPEC structure are the machine names $net \rightarrow src\_mach$, $net \rightarrow dest\_mach$, the directories on each machine $net \rightarrow src\_dir$, $net \rightarrow dest\_dir$, and the names of the input and output files $net \rightarrow iname$, $net \rightarrow oname$ which will be placed in those directories on either machine. The full path-name of the files on machine *a* are $net \rightarrow finame$, $net \rightarrow foname$. These are the concatenation of $net \rightarrow src\_dir$ with $net \rightarrow iname$ or *net →oname* respectively. The string *net →command* may contain a command string to be executed on machine *b* for the current input file. In addition their are flags *net →debug*, *net →save_input*, *net →save_output* to control debugging and automatic deletion of input and output files. Finally there are four function pointers, *net →input_func*, *net →output_func*, *net →send_func*, *net →retrieve_func*, which are called, as described below, to actually create data files or send and receive them. These functions determine the second level communication facilities. Since they are function pointers in the NETSPEC data structure, the second level facilities may be configured dynamically to an appropriate protocol. In particular a single program may simultaneously access two remote machines using completely different low level communications.

In addition to the NETSPEC data structure, three top-level routines are supplied that perform the complete communication task. Each should be supplied with a pointer *net* to a fully initialized NETSPEC data structure. To begin a communication, *create_input* (*net*) is called, which creates an input file with name *net →fname*, on machine *a*, opens it for writing, calls a user supplied routine *net →input_func* (*file ,net*) to write it, and closes the file. The user supplied routine will typically write out a set of numbers and arrays which are the arguments to the subroutine to be executed on the remote machine. The user routine will also write data specifying the application subroutine to run on the remote machine and the type of data transmission involved - formatted or binary - for further details see section 3. Before calling the user supplied routine, nine lines are placed in the file containing the following strings:

> net->src_mach,
> net->dest_mach,
> net->src_dir,
> net->dest_dir,
> net->iname,
> net->oname,
> net->finame,
> net->foname,
> net->command.

These quantities are then available to machine *b* to aid in processing and to provide return addresses for its output data.

To initiate the file transmission, *send_input* (*net*) is called which locates the previously created file *net →fname* on machine *a*, and sends it to machine *b*, placing it in directory *net→dest_dir* with name *net→iname*. The actual file transfer operation is accomplished by a user supplied routine *net→send_func(net)* which allows all system and network dependencies of the file transfer to be separated from the overall communication task. As an example, on 4.2bsd UNIX systems *send_func()* calls the system program *rcp* to transfer the file. The original input file is later deleted unless *net→save_input* is true. It is assumed that a program running on machine b, locates the transferred file, processes it, and places the output in an output file with file name *net→oname*. Whether the output resides on machine a or b will depend on the second level protocol in use. The *command* line in the input file, if non-empty, may be used to indicate a command to be executed on the remote machine.

Finally *retrieve_output(net)* locates the resulting output file and moves it to *net→foname* on machine a, by calling a user supplied routine *net→retrieve_func(net)*. It then opens *net→foname* for reading, calls a user supplied routine *net→output_func(file,net)* to read the file, close the file and delete it unless *net→save_output* is true. As discussed in the following section, the user supplied routines *send_func()* and *retrieve_func()* are not actually written by a user. A library of compatible pairs of such routines is supplied and the user picks a pair that is appropriate for communication between the machines he is using. The other two routines *input_func()* and *output_func()* are written by the user since they describe the data to be exchanged between the machines - see section 3.

2.2. Second Level Communication Protocols

The routines *send_func()* and *retrieve_func()* referred to above are second-level routines which implement the operation of sending and receiving files more or less independently of their contents and without direct interaction with user software. The top level routines assume that the second level routines perform reliably, returning 0 on success or 1 for fatal failures. In particular the fact that a network is unavailable or that a destination machine has crashed is not regarded as a fatal error - the second level routines are expected to deliver data at all costs even if it means waiting a day until a machine comes back up. Since normal communication facilities are generally not reliable enough, the second level routines are built from such standard facilities (third level communications) in such a way as to ensure reliability. Various pairs of these routines are available to implement different communication protocols. We describe one such pair here called *send_func_move* () and *recv_func_move* ().

Send_func_move (*net*) locates a file *net→finame* on machine *a* (presumably previously created by a call to *create_input* ()), and sends it off to machine *b*, directory *net→dest_dir*, filename *net→iname*. Following this, a *signal* file called *net→fisname* is automatically created and shipped to machine *b*, directory *net→dest_dir*, filename *net→isname*. This file contains the names of the input file, output file, source machine, source directory and a return signal filename *net→fosname*, which must be different from *net→fisname*. Both files are sent to the remote machine by calling the operating system to execute a system command called *move* which moves a file to a specified location on a remote machine. It happens that *move* is the name of a system command on all machines on the Los Alamos Computing Network, where we first implemented this software. For other systems we have used *ftp*, *rcp* or *DECNET* to perform the same service. The *move*, *ftp*, *rcp* or *DECNET* call represents the third level in the communication hierarchy. Since reliable file transfers are essential for successful communication, *send_func_move* () is careful to ensure delivery. The return status of the *move* primitive is checked and if the transfer has failed for some reason it is retried later. The initial retry time is 1 second later, but is doubled at every further failure on that file, until the delay time exceeds an hour. After that *move* requests are issued every hour until successful. This deals effectively with either networks or machines that are temporarily down.

Retrieve_move () performs the complementary task of locating a file *net→foname* on machine *a*. This protocol assumes that the *remote* machine will return its output to machine *a*. First it looks for the appearance of the signal file *net→fosname* in the same directory on machine *a* where the input files were created. This is done by entering a non-busy wait loop in which an attempt to open the file is made every 3 seconds. It then locates the output file *net→foname*, and deletes *net→finame*, *net→fisname* and *net→fosname*. If the output file cannot be found immediately after detection of the signal file then a fatal error results.

It can happen that file transfer to the remote machine succeeds but that the remote machine crashes before it can return its output, or while returning its output. To deal with this possibility, the input and signal files are kept on the local machine until *after* the output has been returned to and retrieved by the local machine. In cases of remote system failure, the local machine will be awaiting return of output by looking for the return signal file. Thus it suffices to restart the remote program, and manually move the saved input and signal files from the local to the remote machine. This manual intervention is rare and is a minor inconvenience. Designing an automatic and portable system for detecting remote system failures and restarts seemed too complex. Note that on some systems (e.g. CRAY) input data files transferred before a system crash may actually disappear after restart, depending on the number of hours spanned.

2.3. Signal File Name Space

It is essential to allow the choice of the various filenames used in data transfer to be as flexible as possible. There is a problem in that the remote machine is sitting watching for the arrival of incoming data. It is dangerous to allow it to conclude that any new file created in its directory is an input file. For example the user may also be working on the machine interactively. Thus it is necessary to control in some way the space of allowable file names. With the *send_func_move* () and *recv_func_move* () secondary protocol described above there is a simple solution. The signal filenames are chosen from a limited space whereas data filenames are arbitrary. Our convention is that all input signal filenames are of the form *isig?* where *?* denotes a letter from *a* to *j*. Output signal filenames are of the same form with the initial *i* replaced by *o*. The remote program then sits in a non-busy loop, awakening every 3 seconds to attempt to locate one of the 10 possible filenames (it searches through all 10 possible names, stopping as soon as it finds one). This allows up to 10 applications running on a work-station, or on different work-stations to feed data for processing to the CRAY without fear of collision. A single CRAY program may in fact be processing work for many users on different work-stations. Some care is still needed in the choice of input and output names in the latter cases to avoid collisions between data from different programs or work-stations. This is solved by having each input or output filename end with the same letter as its corresponding signal filename. Similarly since there are 10 possible output signal names, up to 10 different attached processors can be controlled by a single work-station. Should greater parallelism be required, it is trivial to increase the size of the name space, at a small extra cost in searching for incoming files.

3. Data Format and Remote Procedure Calls

Section 2 dealt with the specifics of reliable inter-machine data transfer without discussing the format of the data, or what is done with it. In this section we describe the formats used, the facilities for converting binary data formats between machines and the form of implicit remote procedure call supported by the software.

While the communication software described in section 2 can provide a symmetrical communication between two machines, it is more frequent to use the software in a *master/slave* relationship. In particular it is not necessary for both machines to use all of the software described. As long as there is a program on the slave machine which understands the particular data protocols coming from the master, then successful communication can take place. We have used such master/slave arrangements with the slave understanding only a single communication protocol, on a large number of different machines. One such slave program is so portable that it currently runs on 10 different architectures. We describe the data formats and procedure calls in this more general context.

The program running on the CRAY (slave) consists of three parts: control flow for input file detection, procedure calling and output file dispatch; a set of utility routines for efficient input, output and memory allocation; and a set of user supplied application subroutines covering the range of desired computations. All of these are linked together with the control flow segment to provide a multi-purpose task handler consisting of a single Fortran program. An alternative would have been to use a job control command procedure for file detection which would then run applications as separate processes. We rejected this approach as less portable because of the operating system dependency involved.

The format of the input data file consists of a header containing basic application information, followed by data in the form of integers and floating point numbers, and arrays of each type. The header data includes an integer that specifies which application subroutine is to be called. After opening the input and output files, the control flow routine then calls the requested subroutine with the two open files as arguments. After the subroutine returns, the files are closed, the input files are deleted, and the output is shipped to the requested destination along with an output signal file. The file detection routine then takes over until a new input data file arrives from a remote machine.

As mentioned above, when an application subroutine is called it is provided with two arguments - the open file unit containing its input data and the open file unit in which to place its output. The input file is already wound forward past the header data and so is positioned at the start of the true input data. The input file is actually opened by default for buffered unformatted reading, which is essential to provide optimal efficiency - otherwise is is frequently possible for I/O to dominate computation on a remote vector machine. The input file may be in any format beyond the header area, but typically it is structured as a linear array of data items, to be read in and interpreted by the application subroutine as formal arguments. Special routines are provided to allow binary data from other machines to be read efficiently, see section 3.1. In contrast with normal Fortran calling practice, all arguments are explicitly passed by value - i.e. scalars are supplied as values and vectors are supplied as lists of elements (this is of course essential since a pointer to a memory location on the VAX would be useless on the CRAY). Wherever vectors appear, integer parameters corresponding to their length need to be supplied in previous arguments. It is impossible to predict the memory requirements of the slave program in advance. All memory is allocated dynamically by the application routines and is recaptured when an application has written its output file. Thus the program consumes minimal memory while it is waiting for new data to arrive.

3.1. Binary Data Conversion

Input data arriving from another machine is likely to be in a different format from that used on the CRAY (or other slave). Several possibilities are available. The simplest solution is to send all data as formatted data, i.e. as simple ASCII text. Such data is portable between machines (up to printing round-off effects) but for large volumes of data this is far too inefficient, especially if more than a few digits of precision are required. Alternatively the sending machine (e.g. VAX) may send all data in its standard binary format for each data type. The applications routine on the CRAY then needs to convert this format to the corresponding CRAY data formats before storing the data for processing. Routines to perform such translation are easy to write efficiently using bit manipulation operations on the CRAY and are in fact easily vectorized to support fast translation of long vector arguments. Similarly on output it is advisable for the CRAY to translate data to the VAX binary representations before writing into the output file.

In order to facilitate these translation operations we have written a set of routines on the CRAY for data format conversion between various foreign machine data representations and CRAY data representations. We have used the software to exchange data in binary form between CRAY, ELXSI, VAX, Pyramid, Ridge, Celerity, Masscomp, SUN and Alliant computers. A generic set of routines for converting from IEEE format to VAX or CRAY format handles most new machines. Typical examples of calling sequences for these routines are:

> *subroutine vint(file,n),*
> *subroutine vinta(file,ni,iarray),*
> *subroutine vreal(file,x),*
> *subroutine vreala(file,nf,farray),*

which respectively read and convert to CRAY format an integer n, an integer array *iarray* of length ni, a real number x and a real array *farray* of length nf.

To illustrate the conversion of a VAX 32-bit floating point number to CRAY 64-bit format, we describe the corresponding formats. In the following we regard the last (least significant) bit of a word as bit 0, and we use $[r]$ to denote bit r of a word and $[r-s]$ to denote bits r through s of a word. The VAX floating point format for a non-zero number x then takes the form:

$$x = sign \times fnorm \times 2^{expon} ,$$

where the *sign*, *normalized fraction* and *exponent* are represented as:

$$expon = [22-16][31] -128 ,$$

$$sign = 1 - 2 \times [23] ,$$

$$fnorm = .1[30-24][7-0][15-8] .$$

Note that the leading bit in *fnorm* is NOT represented in hardware. The number 0.0 is represented by an exponent of -128.

A CRAY 64-bit floating point number has a similar 3-part representation where:

$$expon = [62-48] - 16384 ,$$

$$sign = 1 - 2 \times [63] ,$$

$$fnorm = .[47-0] .$$

Thus to convert from VAX 32-bit to CRAY 64-bit floating point we must perform:

$$expon = [22-16]_v [31]_v$$
$$\text{if } expon = 0 \text{ then}$$
$$x = 0$$
$$\text{else}$$
$$[62-48]_c = expon - 128 + 16384$$
$$[63]_c = [23]_v$$
$$[47]_c = 1$$
$$[46-40]_c = [30-24]_v$$
$$[32-39]_c = [7-0]_v$$
$$[31-24]_c = [15-8]_v$$
$$[23-0]_c = 0$$
$$\text{endif}$$

All of these operations may be performed using the standard bit operations on the CRAY, primarily the left and right shift functions $shiftl$() and $shiftr$().

4. Applications

As examples, we have used as the underlying data transfer mechanism file transport primitives from the Los Alamos ICN Network, an Ethernet between mixtures of UNIX and VMS VAXes, DECNET between VMS VAXes and even the UUCP protocol (the last was really just a demonstration).

The original application of this software was the use of a CRAY computer as an attached processor to a VAX as illustrated in Figure 1. We have also permitted a work-station to harness several CRAY computers in parallel as in Figure 3.

As an illustration we have run a program on a network consisting of 3 UNIX and 3 VMS VAXes, a Pyramid and a Celerity 1200 minicomputer, under control of a master program on a Masscomp work-station. This mode of operation is represented by the diagram in Figure 3 with the CRAY computers in that figure replaced by mini-computers.

We routinely use the software to allow programs running on one VAX to access an FPS 164 on another VAX, connected via Ethernet, see Figure 4. The FPS 164 is tightly coupled to a VMS VAX, and in fact FPS does not support this array processor on UNIX mini-computers. This last mode of operation has become our standard working arrangement when running large fluid codes which need to solve linear systems. The software also allows work-stations to access the FPS via the VMS VAX after performing appropriate binary data transformations. We also allow various work-stations and mini-computers to access an Alliant FX-8 multi-processor, to take advantage of its vector and concurrent computation capabilities for compute intensive tasks such as linear equation solution.

5. Conclusions

We have found the concept of treating a powerful supercomputer as an attached processor to be well worth consideration. We believe this trend will become more important in the future as supercomputers become increasingly more specialized. This will decrease their usefulness as general purpose computers and increase the need to provide remote access to a variety of special-purpose hardware. One can envisage a point where users will sit at fast work-stations attached by high-speed communication links to a variety of powerful computing resources including conventional supercomputers, array processors, systolic arrays and massively parallel computers. Work-station programs would then avail of these resources as needed as well as providing the user with the intrinsic benefits of a work-station such as fast graphics, window managers, high quality software environments and non-timeshared interactive cycles.

In fact while we are enthusiastic about the future of massively parallel computation (thousands or millions of processors), see for example[3], we doubt that machines with very large numbers of processors make sense other than as attached processors. Such machines have fundamental scalar bottlenecks which will force scalar computation to be performed elsewhere.

Acknowledgement

We would like to thank Los Alamos National Laboratory for providing access to its CRAY super-computers and ICN computer network, and for the direct support of C-Division at LANL where much of this work was carried out.

References

1.   O. McBryan, Los Alamos National Laboratory Annual Report, 1983.

2.   O. McBryan, "A UNIX Interface to Supercomputers," in *Proceedings of the ARO Conference on Microcomputers in Large Scale Scientific Computation*, ed. A. Wouk, SIAM, Philadelphia.

3.   O. McBryan, "The Connection Machine: PDE Solution on 65536 Processors," Los Alamos National Laboratory Preprint, Aug 1986.

A UNIX Interface to Supercomputers[*]

OLIVER A. MCBRYAN[†]

Abstract. We describe a convenient interface between UNIX-based work-stations or minicomputers, and supercomputers such as the CRAY series machines. Using this interface, the user can issue commands entirely on the UNIX system, with remote compilation, loading and execution performed on the supercomputer. The interface is not a remote login interface. Rather the domain of various UNIX utilities such as compilers, archivers and loaders are extended to include the supercomputer. The user need know essentially nothing about the supercomputer operating system, commands or filename restrictions. Standard UNIX utilities will perform supercomputer operations transparently. UNIX command names and arguments are mapped to corresponding supercomputer equivalents, suitable options are selected as needed, UNIX directory tree filenames are coerced to allowable supercomputer names and all source and output files are automatically transferred between the machines.

The primary purpose of the software is to allow the programmer to benefit from the interactive features of UNIX systems including screen editors, software maintenance utilities such as *make* and *SCCS,* and various text manipulation utilities. The interface was designed particularly to support development of very large multi-file programs, possibly consisting of hundreds of files and hundreds of thousands of lines of code. All supercomputer source is kept on the work-station.

---

[*] Research supported in part by DOE contract DE-ACO2-76ER03077 and by NSF grant DMS-83-12229.
[†] C-3, MS-B265, Los Alamos National Laboratory, Los Alamos, NM 87545.
  Permanent address: Courant Institute, 251 Mercer Street, New York, NY 10012.

1. Introduction

We have developed UNIX-based software which provides a UNIX workstation or minicomputer user with transparent access to a CRAY or other supercomputer. Effectively, we extend the domain of certain UNIX utilities to the supercomputer. It is assumed that there is a direct connection between the workstation and the super-computer. The connection should be high-speed for reasonable efficiency since remote source file transfers are involved. Facilities supported include remote compilation, linking and execution, along with data retrieval.

The goal of the software described here is to allow the user to develop new programs entirely in a UNIX work-station environment. Once fully developed, the programs are generally run directly on the CRAY, although remote execution is also available.

The primary observation that led to development of this software was that 95% of our CRAY program development time was involved with routine editing, debugging and compilation activities. Most of these activities are best performed on a work-station. For example, powerful software maintenance utilities such as *make* and *SCCS* are not available on the CRAY, and can greatly speed the program development effort, especially for large multi-file programs. As a direct application, we can now use *make* to maintain large programs on the CRAY.

There are many additional advantages to distributed program development. The workstation user can avail of full interactivity, to an extent not available on super-computers. In particular one typically finds faster response on work-stations to interrupt-driven facilities such as editors. Various powerful software tools, including screen editors, high-level languages and transformational utilities are available on work-stations. Furthermore by off-loading interactive activity, the supercomputer is freed for batch processing, which is where it performs best. In many cases the work-station may also be used effectively for graphical post-processing of data returned from the supercomputer.

Section 2 provides an overview of the facilities supported by the interface software. Section 3 describes in detail the filename coercion facilities that are used to map the UNIX filename space into the more restrictive filename space of the supercomputer. Sections 4, 5 and 6 describe the mapping of basic compilation utilities to their CRAY equivalents. Finally section 7 discusses extension of the domain of the *make* utility to include the supercomputer.

2. Scope and Facilities

We will discuss the UNIX interface in terms of CRAY computers running the CTSS operating system, although we have implemented a similar interface to the COS operating system. The general mechanism is clearly extendible to other super-computers. The network connection between the supercomputer and the work-station is also a factor - we discuss here the use of facilities of the Los Alamos Integrated Computing Network. However the network facilities required are so simple that a similar system could likely be built on top of any reasonable network. In fact, the existence of a file transfer protocol would suffice, using software we have described in a related paper[1].

The fundamental approach we have taken is to implement only the most fre-quently used CRAY utilities as UNIX utilities. Shell command files are created that implement the desired CRAY commands as UNIX utilities, taking standard UNIX arguments, options and filenames. These command files map the UNIX commands into their corresponding CRAY equivalents, supply the appropriate options to the CRAY command, arrange that any file arguments are transferred to the CRAY, and when everything is in place, execute the correct CRAY command on the remote machine. After command execution, any output or error messages are returned to the work-station and are directed to the user's standard output.

An important aspect of the steps described above is the transfer of files. File formats usually need to be modified on each side before and after transfer. More significantly, the supercomputer and work-station will generally use different file name spaces. To provide maximum generality we provide for filename coercion between the systems. The filename coercion facilities are the same among the vari-ous basic utilities. Furthermore uniform conventions are adopted for file location. All source files (including assembler) are kept on the UNIX machine while all object, library and executables are kept on the CRAY. Readable output files such as assem-bler source or compiler listings are returned with an appropriate name to the UNIX machine. In cases where files are returned, the inverse of the filename coercion func-tion is applied providing a reasonable UNIX expansion. We discuss all of these issues in more detail below.

In our case the most important target utilities are the CRAY Fortran compiler *CFT*, the CRAY C compiler *CC*, the CRAY assembler *CAL*, the CRAY loader *LDR*, and the CRAY Librarian *BUILD*. The corresponding UNIX utilities are the *f77, cc, ar* and *ld* programs. Thus we discuss these cases in most detail. Higher level UNIX utilities such as *make* generally issue commands to low level utilities such as those described above. By developing UNIX compatible utilities that call the corresponding CRAY utilities we therefore effectively extend the domain of *make* to the CRAY.

While the functionality of basic non-interactive utilities tend to map rather well across systems, it frequently happens that a CRAY utility may require an option that has no corresponding UNIX equivalent (see below for examples). In these cases an extra UNIX option is added to the standard UNIX utility argument list. The result is that even a naive user can compile and link CRAY programs without ever logging into the CRAY or reading any CRAY manual, using the same commands or makefiles he would use on a UNIX machine. Occasionaly an extra option or two may be required in order to support some special CRAY feature, but these do not appear in normal usage.

3. Filename Coercion

CRAY CTSS filenames may contain at most 8 characters, whereas UNIX filenames may have essentially arbitrary length, including a directory part. Similar restrictions are found on many other supercomputer operating systems. Each UNIX filename to be compiled should be alphanumeric apart from a directory prefix and a suffix consisting of *.c*, *.f*, *.s*, *.o* or *.a*. We refer to the filename with the directory prefix and the suffix removed as the file *base name*. The directory prefix will be stripped, but remembered, before sending files to the CRAY. Similarly characters beyond 7 in the base name are stripped, the period is deleted from the suffix but the remaining suffix character is maintained. Consequently the CRAY file name always ends in the same suffix character as the UNIX filename. As examples, */usr/me/short.c* maps into the CRAY name *shortc*, while */usr/me/longname.c* would become *longnamc*. One exception to this rule is that library archive base names are truncated to 8 characters and no suffix is added. This is because typically certain system-supplied CRAY libraries will be required, and will normally not have names ending in *a*. Thus the UNIX archive file */usr/me/mygoodlib.a* would be represented on the CRAY as the library file *mygoodli*.

In cases such as listing, preprocessor output or assembler files which are generated on the CRAY, files are returned with an inverse coercion rule applied. Such files will be placed in the current working directory with the full basename and an appropriate suffix of *.l*, *.e* or *.s* respectively.

In addition to filename coercion, certain other transformations may be required in exchanging files between the CRAY and work-station. For example, on the Los Alamos network a uniform *standard text* file format, (*stext*), is supported to provide portability between machines. However on each individual machine it is necessary to convert files from *stext* form to the *native text* form for that machine, *ntext*, before processing by editors, compilers or other utilities on the machine. System programs *stext* and *ntext* are supplied to convert a native text file on any machine to standard text format and to convert a standard text file to native text format, respectively. Our software automatically performs these format transformations when exchanging text files between machines of differing architectures. All text files will always be converted into native text form on the machine they reside on.

There is a difference in the treatment of source and object filenames which are provided as arguments to supported utilities. Source, including assembler, filename arguments to utilities (suffixes *.c*, *.f* or *.s*) cause the corresponding UNIX files to be sent to the CRAY with filename coercion as above, as well as appropriate text format transformation between native text modes. Object or library filename arguments (suffixes *.o* or *.a*) are interpreted differently. Each *.o* or *.a* file argument is interpreted as denoting a *previously compiled* file or a previously built library *on the CRAY*. The corresponding CRAY object or library filename is obtained using the rules described above. The rationale here is that there seems little point in moving such object files back to the workstation. They are regarded as conceptually residing on the work-station, however, in that utilities behave in the same way they would if the files had been stored there. In fact the compile utilities *ccc*, *cft* and *car* described below create dummy object or archive files on the work-station corresponding to each file compiled. These dummy files carry the names one would expect on a UNIX system, i.e. filename coercion is not applied, and their main purpose is to provide a map of the current compilation state on the CRAY, including information about the exact compilation time of each CRAY file.

4. The CCC command

The UNIX version of the CRAY C compile command is called *ccc* to distinguish it from the standard UNIX C compiler *cc*. However *ccc* takes the same standard arguments that the *cc* command takes, along with some CRAY specific ones. The calling sequence is:

ccc [-c] [-o name] [-E] [-O] [-Dstring] .. [-Ustring] .. [-Istring] ..
[-ic] [-l] [-V] [-p priority] [-r] file1 file2 ..

The −*c* option specifies compile only, without loading.

The −*o* option assigns the following name to the compiled program.

The −*E* option runs the C preprocessor on each C file leaving the output in the current directory with suffix *.e* .

The −*O* option is ignored.

The −*Idir* option specifies a search directory for include files.

The −*Dstring* and −*Ustring* options implement preprocessor defines and undefines as in the UNIX C compiler.

The −*pc* option specifies that the C pre-processor is to be executed on the CRAY. The default is to execute the pre-processor on the work-station.

The −*l* option places full listing files in the current directory with suffix *.l* .

The −*V* option specifies that all C sources files are to be compiled specially with the *varargs* mechanism.

The −*p* option specifies that CRAY compilation or loading is to be performed at the specified priority level.

The −*r* option causes the compiled program to be run on the CRAY and the output transferred to the UNIX standard output.

The last five options, −*ic* , −*l* , −*V* , −*p* and −*r* are not standard UNIX facilities. They provide access to desirable CRAY C features. In particular the CRAY C compiler requires a special argument −*V* if a source file containing a subroutine with a variable number of arguments is to be compiled. It is also useful to see the CRAY compiler listing - if the $-l$ option is supplied then for each compiled source file, a corresponding CRAY listing file will be returned to the UNIX machine with the same filename, but suffix $.l$.

Filenames ending in $.c$, $.f$, $.s$, $.o$ or $.a$ are assumed to be C source, Fortran source, CAL assembler, previously compiled CRAY object files or CRAY library archives of object files respectively. Each source file is converted to standard text format, moved to the remote machine, converted to native text and compiled. Thus *lusr/me/longname.c* is moved to *longnamc* on the CRAY and is compiled to produce *longnamo*. If a listing file is requested it is returned as *longname.l* to UNIX. After each file is compiled, a corresponding dummy file with suffix $.o$ is created in the current directory to record the compilation status and time of compilation on the CRAY. In the above example a dummy file *longname.o* would be created on the work-station.

One issue not discussed so far is the use of the C pre-processor. Since the pre-processor is simply a text transformer, it may obviously be executed either on the work-station or on the CRAY. The $-pc$ option is provided to allow the user to choose either possibility. The choice made affects primarily the outcome of the C *include* facility. Depending on which route is taken, file inclusion will be performed either on the CRAY or on the work-station. It is more consistent with our general goals if file inclusion is performed on the work-station - include files are after all text files. However if this is done, certain precautions are required. For example, there are system include files such as *<stdio.h>* which are used by many programs, but are very system-dependent. It would be incorrect to include a work-station version of such a file in source code targeted for the CRAY. Consequently a seperate directory of CRAY system include files must be maintained on the work-station, and searched by the pre-processor before it searches the standard system directory. This is easily accomplished in practice using the $-I$ include directory option.

One further pre-processing step is automatically inserted by the *ccc* command, and is provided for two reasons. A disadvantage of the distributed compilation discussed here is that there is delay involved while waiting for files to be transferred to the CRAY. It is therefore very desirable to minimize the length of source files. Secondly, the CRAY C compiler has difficulty with long lines in source files. We handle both of these issues by subjecting each source file to a filter called *shorten* before sending it. This step is performed after pre-processing, if that was requested on the work-station. The *shorten* filter replaces consecutive white-space characters found outside of quotes by a single space, and then folds every line after 79 characters, taking care not to split strings.

If loading is not suppressed by the $-c$ option, then both the newly compiled files and the previously compiled files, represented by any *.o* file arguments, are loaded together along with requested libraries. The resulting executable image is called *name* if the *-o name* option was used, or *a.out* otherwise. Any unrecognized command line arguments are assumed to be options for the CRAY loader. This allows various special facilities to be accessed, for example a dynamic array may be specified in this way to facilitate programs that perform internal storage allocation.

If the $-r$ option was specified on the compile line, the compiled program is run and its output returned to the standard output of the UNIX work-station.

5. The CFT Command

The *CFT* command allows Fortran source files to be compiled on a CRAY. The usage is similar to that for the *ccc* command, but with fewer options supported:

cft [-c] [-o name] [-l] [-r] file1.f file2.f filer.o ..

The $-c$ option specifies compilation only.

The $-o$ option assigns the following name to the program.

The $-l$ option places full listing files in filei.l.

The $-r$ option causes the program to be run on the CRAY after loading.

File name coercion, and text file format transformations, are performed in the same way as for the *CCC* command. Thus each Fortran source file (suffix *.f*) is converted to standard text, moved to the remote machine, converted to native text and compiled. The filename file.f will produce a CRAY source file called filef, and a binary file called fileo. The listing file, if requested, is returned to the current directory as file.l. After each file is compiled, a corresponding dummy file with suffix *.o* is created in the current directory on the work-station to record the compilation status and time of compilation on the CRAY. Each object file argument (suffix *.o*) to *cft* is interpreted as denoting a previously compiled object file on the CRAY.

If loading is not suppressed by the −c option, then both the newly compiled files and previously compiled files are loaded together and the executable image is named file1x, (derived from the first filename argument), or 'name' if the −o option was used. Any remaining command-line arguments are passed to the CRAY loader as arguments.

6. The *CAR* Command

The *CAR* command accesses the CRAY Librarian, *BUILD*, using the standard argument syntax of the UNIX *ar* archive program.

$$car \quad option \quad libname \quad file1.o \quad file2.o \quad ..$$

Here *option* is one of *c*, *r*, *t* or *x* denoting respectively *create* a new archive, *replace* files in a library, *list* the table of contents of a library or *extract* all files from a library. Filename coercion follows the rules given earlier in section 3. Thus both the archive name *libname* and the object filenames *filei.o* are subjected to directory and name truncation. All of the resulting object files are assumed to exist on the CRAY and the resulting archive file is also left on the CRAY. After the archive file is created or updated on the CRAY a corresponding dummy file with suffix *.a* is created in the current directory on the work-station to record the archive status and time of archiving on the CRAY.

7. Using MAKE on the CRAY

The real payoff for the development of the facilities described in the previous sections comes when they are coupled with the UNIX *make* program. *Make* is a utility used to maintain software projects. It deals with the mechanics of assembling large programs from many inter-related source files. The user specifies how to build the program by supplying an appropriate set of commands in a *makefile*. *Make* reads the *makefile*, checks to see what commands remain to be executed to build the required object, and performs these. An important point is that *make* attempts to perform the minimal amount of work necessary to build a program. This is accomplished by using a set of built in dependency rules. For example, *make* realizes that an object file *file.o* is obtained from a source file *file.c* or *file.f*. If *make* is required to create an object file *file.o* as part of building a program, it first checks to see if a corresponding source file *file.c* or *file.f* is available. If so, it compares the date of last modification of the source code file and the last version of the object file (if there is one). If the source code was modified *since* the object file, or if no object file is present, then *make* automatically calls the appropriate compiler command on the source file; otherwise no action is performed by *make* for that object file. For further information about *make* see the UNIX operating system user manuals[2]. For the discussion here we note one other feature of *make*: the built in rules for creating object files from dependencies are easily modified. For example, the rule for creating *file.o* from *file.c* looks like:

$$\$(CC) \ \$(CFLAGS) \ file.c$$

Here *CC* and *CCFLAGS* are make macro variables that define the compiler command and compiler options to be used in compiling file.c, while $\$(\cdot)$ denotes macro variable evaluation. Both are given default values by *make*: $CC = cc$ and $CFLAGS = -c$ respectively. Similarly, the default rules for compiling Fortran programs involve macro variables $F77$ and *FFLAGS*, which have default values of $f77$ and $-c$, while the rules for creating a library use a default variable *AR* with default value *ar*.

Suppose that we have a large multi-file, and possibly multi-directory, program maintained for compilation by *make*. Normally the program will be developed and debugged on the work-station. A version for the supercomputer may be maintained from the same source files by using conditional compilation. In this context the C pre-processor makes an excellent pre-processor for both Fortran and C. We have used it to maintain portable source code for more than 10 machines within a single software version.

Once the work-station version of the program is ready, a supercomputer compilation may be made from the same directory and makefile by simply redefining the *make* variables *CC*, $F77$ and *AR* to the values *ccc*, *cft* and *car* respectively. If necessary, the variables *CFLAGS* and *FFLAGS* may be set to record any special options required such as listing files or to request the $-V$ option for variable-number-of-argument routines in C. Conditional compilation may also be effected at this point by adding the appropriate conditional compilation flags to *CFLAGS*. *Make* then takes over, issuing all needed instructions for the complete compilation and linking of the program on the CRAY, including handling all of the issues of file transfer and name coercion. While object and library files are not kept on the work-station, the dummy versions of such files are created by the compilers as discussed previously and record faithfully the correct last time of compilation of the corresponding files on the CRAY.

One major inconvenience is that under CTSS and other supercomputer operating systems frequently a user's files are deleted within 24 hours of logging out. As a result it is generally necessary to save all files on the CRAY to a mass storage system before logging off. This is in fact easily automated using a *save* entry in the work-station makefile, which simply looks at the current list of *.o* and *.a* files on the work-station, and sends commands to the CRAY to save those files as well as the corresponding source files. At the next work-station session a *restore* entry in the makefile may be activated to return the CRAY files from storage to the CRAY. However none of these steps involves any actions to the work-station files. The times recorded will still be those for the original CRAY compilation, avoiding the necessity for any unnecessary recompilation.

References

1. O. McBryan, "Using Supercomputers as Attached Processors," in *Proceedings of the ARO Conference on Microcomputers in Large Scale Scientific Computation*, ed. A. Wouk, SIAM, Philadelphia.

2. *The UNIX Users's Manual Reference Guide*, USENIX Association, 1984.

What Kind of Workstation Should I Buy?
Seven-Fold Criteria for Hardware and Software

L. RIDGWAY SCOTT*

ABSTRACT

The problem of designing a workstation suitable for an individual scientist or group of scientists will be addressed from an abstract point of view. A set of seven criteria concerning hardware are presented that should be considered when assessing one's needs and comparing various available products. Seven categories of software are also discussed that are critical for someone doing code development, testing and production runs on a remote computer (mainframe or supercomputer). The criteria discussed are intended to be a model checklist relevant especially for people doing code development and production work in scientific computation. After discussing criteria for evaluating workstations, two examples are given of inexpensive yet powerful systems that should be possible to assemble today.

People doing scientific computation are faced with a bewildering situation when they begin to purchase a workstation to help with the development and testing of codes and the interpretation of data from production runs. This technology is evolving so rapidly that choices are often not clear cut. One is constantly bombarded with claims and counter claims, and there is a real danger of designing a system using pieces of hardware or software that turn out to be "vaporware." I have been asked on a number of occasions by friends, colleagues and administrators to answer the question posed in the title, and this note presents the issues I see as being most important. The problem of designing a workstation suitable for an individual scientist or group of scientists will be addressed from a fairly abstract point of view. A set of seven criteria concerning hardware are presented that should be considered when assessing one's needs and comparing various available products. The seven criteria are an expansion of the 5M criterion of Dick Phillips of the University of Michigan, the 4M machine related to the SPICE project at

* Department of Mathematics, University of Michigan, Ann Arbor, MI 48109-1092.

Carnegie-Mellon [2] and the 3M workstation concept under development at Brown University [3]. Seven categories of software are also discussed that are critical for someone doing code development, testing and production runs on a remote computer (mainframe or supercomputer). It is especially important to consider software as an integral part of the workstation; frequently too little money is budgeted for software, and the potential value of the workstation is not realized. The criteria discussed here do not exhaust all possibilities, nor are all of them critical to everyone. They are intended to be a model checklist relevant especially for people doing code development and production work in scientific computation. After discussing criteria for evaluating workstations, I will give two examples of inexpensive yet powerful systems that should be possible to assemble today.

Hardware

There are (at least) seven variables that are important to consider regarding hardware when designing a scientific computing workstation. They are all quantitative in nature, and we shall try to weight them so that an ideal system has all variables of order unity. We are therefore prejudicing the discussion to a nontrivial degree with our own preferential weights for the various categories, and individuals should not be intimidated by someone else's large need in a specific area. There is no need to feel that having ANY of the variables ≥ 1 is necessary, as a small personal workstation with a good balance could be just as useful as a more powerful one that must be shared. In any case, if the budget is limited, there may be no other choice. The seven-vector X we use to describe a workstation has the components x_1, x_2, ..., x_7 which indicate that the system

executes x_1 million instructions per second,

performs x_2 million FLOPS (floating-point operations per second),

has a bus that transfers x_3 million words per second,

has x_4 million words of program/data memory,

has x_5 million bytes of (raster) graphics display memory,

has x_6 million lines of disc storage

and can communicate with its neighbors at x_7 million bits per second.

Some words of explanation are in order concerning items 5 and 6.

Raster graphics memory can be allocated in two ways: for spatial resolution or for color resolution. Using anti-aliasing techniques, these are somewhat interchangeable. For example, one could have a one-megabyte display with the following possibilities:

pixel resolution	number of colors
2K by 2K	four
1K by 1K	256
512 by 512	full color (32 bit-planes)

Graphics displays with the latter two sets of parameters are now commonly available. Certain displays are software switchable between these two options. By "full color," we mean a color resolution that is sufficient to reproduce typical photographs to an accuracy acceptable to most humans. Actually, 24 bits per pixel are considered sufficient for this purpose. The intensity variations allowed by a large number of colors permit the increase of apparent spatial accuracy by a method known as anti-aliasing. A straight line drawn nearly parallel to one of the axes displays noticable "jaggies" which can be reduced by making neighboring pixels interpolate (in color space) between the colors of the background and line.

One area in which current workstation specifications are often deficient is that of graphics display resolution. It used to be very expensive to get one-megabyte displays, but they are now quite reasonably priced, as will be pointed out below. Also, graphics software has achieved an admirable level of standardization, so the inexpensive frame buffers need not be user-unfriendly. Graphics equipment can still be very expensive, but the expense is related to the speed of redrawing (e.g., in rotating a three-dimensional object). However, if speed is not critical, good resolution can be obtained on a moderate budget.

By "lines" of disc storage, we simply mean that a line should be thought of as 80 characters (or equivalently, 80 bytes). Thus $x_6 = 1$ means an 80 megabyte hard disc. The transfer rate for data to and from the hard disc is also an important consideration in many cases. It may also be closely related to the value of x_3.

Items 1-3 are obviously tightly coupled. If x_1 or x_3 is small, it will be hard for x_2 to be very large. Typical number-crunching algorithms have two arithmetic operations per data transfer (cf. the architecture of the Cray 1), so one would expect $x_2 \leq 2x_3$ in general. Array processors offer the hope of high-performance computation at low cost, but the bus-transfer (or other method of data-transfer) rate is critical. An excellent set of benchmarks has been compiled by Jack Dongarra [1] that compare x_2 for the entire gamut of computers, from PC's to supercomputers, on some computationally intensive problems.

We have left out of the criterion vector X some important hardware considerations, namely the number of bits in the addressing scheme, virtual memory and word length. There are essentially only two common choices of addressing mode: 32-bit or 24-bit. (Anything less that this can be criticized today as a severe architectural limitation.) Obviously 32-bit addressing is preferable, as 24-bit addressing limits total (even virtual) memory to 16 megabytes (for byte addressing). Virtual memory allows addressing of more core memory than is physically available, utilizing disk space for the auxiliary memory and swapping things into core as needed. It is of value both for simulating computations on larger machines and simply for doing large computations that do not require all of the data to be in core at once. For certain scientific calculations, having virtual memory is critical, and in this case the data-transfer rate for the hard disc should be evaluated very carefully. Virtual memory is, in part, also a software issue, and so it will be mentioned subsequently with regard to operating systems. Another important hardware issue is the (floating point) word-length. Again there are typically two possibilities, 32-bit and 64-bit. For program development and testing, it is arguable that 32 bits suffice, as long as double-precision is at least available in software. However, this situation may be different for different individuals, and it may change in the near future.

Let us give some simple examples of how the above criteria are used. If one is interested primarily in code development, with little need for sophisticated graphical interpretation of data from production runs, then variables one through four are of most importance. On the other hand, someone working with standard software computing on a remote supercomputer might simply need a workstation for interpretation of computational results. In this case, variables four through six are perhaps more important than one or two. The role of variable three for graphics work depends strongly on what is being done; if entire images need to be transferred from memory to the screen, x_3 needs to be very large. In a working situation where one is alone (and say using remote supercomputers via a modem), variable seven may not be critical. But for a group that needs to exchange software, data, etc., frequently between workstations, variable seven ought to be close to unity, if not significantly higher. There is no simple formula for the exact relationship between all of these variables that one can give for all situations. My contention is that each individual (or individual working group) should determine personal weights $W = (w_1, w_2, ..., w_7)$ regarding the relative value of each of these variables and then solve the linear programming problem:

$$\text{maximize} \quad W^T X \quad \text{subject to}$$

the cost of the system X being within budget.

And there may be other factors to be included in the model. It is more important to get a balance of what one needs than to maximize any particular variable. It is certainly feasible to design a workstation around a standard PC for about \$5K with such a balance (but with each $x_i << 1$). It is better to have something that satisfies all of your needs to some degree (albeit slowly) than to give up completely on any important variable.

There are several necessary peripherals not covered by the variable X. Hardcopy devices have dropped in price dramatically recently. Dot-matrix, ink-jet and laser printers offer varying degrees of quality for corresponding prices. Some of these devices allow a limited number of colors. In picking a plain-paper printer, one should consider carefully whether it is compatible with the various software (e.g., for typesetting and graphics) that may want to use it. Pen plotters are now available for around $1K that allow multiple pens (and therefore multiple colors) and high spatial resolution of one-thousandth of an inch. For some color graphics applications, it may be advisable to get a separate video printer; models capable of making both 35mm slides and 3 by 4 Polaroids at 1K by 1K resolution are now available for about $5K. Modems are also now quite inexpensive and are essential for communication with the rest of the world, if one is not hard-wired to a high-speed network such as ARPANET (which is of course preferable). If large data files are to be stored on the workstation disk, a tape (or laser-disk) back-up system is advisable. Other peripherals that may be useful are "mice," digitizers, "joy sticks," track-balls, voice input/output, and so on.

There is a hidden issue concerning cost of workstations, namely, maintenance contracts. Many of the more powerful workstations require agreements amounting (usually) to about one percent of the list price of the equipment per month, even if it has been bought at a substantial discount. In some cases at academic institutions, this can mean that one pays the same amount for maintenance over a four year period as the original purchase price. This is not the case for more popular computers targeted primarily for the business market (i.e., PC's). We are not arguing that the maintenance costs are not justifiable; indeed, to budget nothing for this item is imprudent even if not required. However, one needs to be aware that the true cost of equipment itself involves two variables, the initial cost and the maintenance cost.

There is another hidden cost related to workstations, namely, the time spent in system management. This can vary from reading the manuals to learn how to format a floppy disc for a PC to complex and time consuming tasks on larger systems that border on the running of a small computer center. The latter certainly is characteristic of a "departmental VAX" and is best done by a dedicated staff person. Even a network of workstations requires a person to be designated "system manager." This person will have to assign sign-on id's and passwords, allocate disc space, back up disc files periodically, install new software, educate new users, and so on. If salary money is not allocated for an appropriate person to fill this role, scientific staff best suited for other tasks will end up having to perform it. This can be a significant waste of human resources.

Software

Software for a workstation is a critical consideration. It is omitted from X because it is hard to quantify, but there are certainly workstations with a lot of software and ones with little. I will try to list important categories of software, without mentioning brand names, and give important considerations where possible. These are as follows:

1. operating system: virtual memory, multi-tasking, multi-user, supports windows?

2. standard ASCII word-processor: full-screen editor, has macros?

3. language compilers: Ada, Algol, APL, Basic, C, Fortran, Forth, Lisp, Pascal, PL/I?

4. communications software: file transfer?

5. graphics packages: standard graphics-terminal emulation?

6. mathematical word-processor or typesetting system: can do all symbols and character sets, has macros?

7. database management

Some explanations of the concepts involved and how the software is used are in order.

A multi-tasking operating system is one that can do more than one thing at once, and a multi-user one allows more than one person to be using the computer at once. Multiple "windows" facilitate keeping track of the various tasks one is doing, by allowing a different "window" for each job on different parts of the screen. A typical situation in code development might be as follows. In debugging or modifying a code to run on a supercomputer, the code is broken into different parts. Imagine the eager programmer who is editing one subroutine while compiling another locally to check for errors. In addition, previously edited and compile-checked routines are being sent over a network to the supercomputer. And data from previous runs could be on the way back. Not to mention a printing job of some sort that is going on as well. Only the compilation is truly computationally intensive; the other tasks involve a great deal of waiting by the cpu and thus can be handled easily without degrading compile time significantly, provided the operating system supports multi-tasking.

The way to write code today is via a word-processing system. It should allow full-screen editing (as opposed to line editing), i.e., to change something just rub out the old and type in the new, with arrow keys governing the movement of the cursor. The ability to copy, move, search and replace are all fairly standard on a wide range of systems. Not so universal are macros, the ability to define some simple symbol to mean a (possibly very long) series of keystrokes. If there is anything that you do repeatedly (and there usually is!), macros can be a big help.

Local language compliers are essential for efficient code debugging even if running programs remotely. It may be useful to have more than one compiler, one that compiles quickly and another that compiles (more slowly) into quick code. Compilers with interactive debuggers are also widely available. Moreover, it may be useful to have compliers for additional languages handy for doing different tasks. For example, graphing some preliminary results might be done most easily in Basic, and writing complicated graphics routines might be best done in C. And a symbol-manipulation program might require a Lisp complier, or one might choose APL for doing complex algebra. Forth is apparently a very useful language in many contexts, especially for control of laboratory equipment. These are but a few simple examples to indicate how a need for different language compilers might arise.

A communications program should allow you to compute remotely as easily as possible. For example, you should be able to record on disk all that transpired during a session. A critical need is the ability to do "file transfer," which means to transmit a file and to check for errors in transmission as the transfer proceeds (with provision for automatic retransmission if errors are detected). To a large extent, this depends not just on the local workstation, but also on the remote computer system and the telecommunications network that is used. Thus one may need several programs for use with different remote computational systems (one of which could be your local mainframe).

A word-processing system that allows mathematical symbols is not strictly needed for Fortran programming, although it is now possible (e.g., via the WEB system) to write code documentation in natural mathematical symbols. However, preparation of papers for publication is certainly one of a scientist's major tasks, and a workstation should address all needs at once. Similarly, a data-base management program may look out of place, but it can be very useful for mailing lists, bibliographies, etc., at minimal additional cost.

In looking at the list of software, I hope it will become apparent that one should budget a fair amount of money for software. And keep some aside to buy new software as it comes along (this should be thought of as the cost of software maintenance). We have listed seven major categories of software; each of these might represent several packages in itself. Moreover, there will undoubtedly be things of interest to others not listed here. For example, a spreadsheet program is very useful when purchasing further computer systems and can be used in other productive ways as well. Another type of software mentioned by participants at the workshop might be characterized as "productivity tools" or "problem-solving environments." Examples might be things like TKSolver for a PC or MACSYMA on a larger machine (or their many competitors). Software of this type discussed at this workshop include the communications/graphics package of McBryan and the CLAM system described by Gropp.

New Directions

Although we know of no $X = (1, 1, ..., 1)$ workstation for under $50K, we claim it ought to be possible to construct one, either now or in the near future. Moreover, it is possible to assemble inexpensive systems that have some of these capabilities now, and this represents a major improvement in the price/performance ratio for scientific workstations. Let us consider two examples to illustrate this point. All figures will be approximate, and no vendor names will be given in order to avoid slighting anyone by omission due to my ignorance.

An impressive graphics workstation can be constructed using a lowly PC by adding available single cards containing graphics frame-buffers as follows:

megabytes of display memory	cost
1.0	$5K
0.5	$2.K
0.25	$2K

These boards come with basic software (GKS primitives, Tektronix emulation, etc.) Corresponding high-resolution monitors can be bought starting around $1K (for 512 by 512 resolution).

For number-crunching applications, array processor boards are available for the VME bus that have peak computational rates of roughly 15 megaFLOPS (million floating point operations per second) in the price range of $15K, or one thousand FLOPS per dollar. It is interesting to note that both the Cray 1 and the IBM/PC with an 8087 math co-processor chip yield performance/price ratios of about ten FLOPS per dollar (error bars: a factor of three!). While it is apparently difficult to achieve these peak speeds in general calculations, it should be possible to get multi-megaFLOPS performance relatively cheaply. Moreover, such a computational environment more closely approximates the one that would be used for production runs (e.g., on a Cray or Cyber/ETA machine), and thus would be very useful in the program development and testing stage.

Conclusions

I have listed seven criteria for both hardware and software that are important to consider in designing a workstation for code development and graphical interpretation of data. These variables will affect the overall efficiency of a system, but the true variable of interest is the "throughput" on the problems you wish to solve. Benchmarks are needed for typical tasks, in addition to number-crunching. One might be based on the scenario given above regarding the need for a multi-tasking environment, in which a compilation, file transfer, production run, graphics calculation, printing job and editing are all going on simultaneously. Ideally, you would have the opportunity to try out a system before buying to see how well it fits your needs. One thing to keep in mind, however, is that a workstation changes how one approaches problems, and even the choice of problems. Thus you should choose a workstation that will lead you in a research direction that you want to go, not just get one that appears to automate the tasks you are currently performing.

References

[1] J. J. DONGARRA, *Performance of various computers using standard linear equation software in a Fortran environment*, Technical Memorandum No. 23, Mathematics and Computer Science Division, Argonne National Laboratory, 17 June 1985.

[2] S. E. FAHLMAN and S. P. HARBISON, *The SPICE Project*, in D. R. Barstow, H. E. Shrobe and E. Sandewall, eds., **Interactive Programming Environments**, McGraw-Hill, New York, 198.

[3] E. FOSTER, *Profs demand cheap super PCs*, **Infoworld 7**, no. 18 (6 May 1985), p. 22.